COLLEGE

—•IN•—

FOUR YEARS

MAKING EVERY SEMESTER COUNT

GRANVILLE M. SAWYER JR., PH.D.

ISBN: 978-0-9916143-0-1

About the Author

For more than three decades, I have been doing what I love – helping students have successful college experiences. I've had the great privilege to work with more than 10,000 students at universities, both public and private, on large and small campuses.

My students have learned from me and I have also learned a great deal from them. One of my most important roles as an educator is to listen to their experiences and exchange with them advice and insights I have gained over the years.

Students would frequently tell me, "Doc you should write this stuff down." Well, I finally took their advice, **College in Four Years** *is a compilation of stories that illustrate the insights my students found most useful.*

I am an educator but I am truly a storyteller at heart. Both titles are the direct result of my parents, both educators and great storytellers. My father (a university president) and my mother (an English professor) shared advice and insights with me in the same way I do with students – they shared their stories. Like my parents did for me and I did for my daughters, **College in Four Years***, gives me the opportunity to offer more students clear advice based on our experiences. No sermons or lectures, just real stories and the lessons that helped students succeed.*

Dr. Granville M. Sawyer, Jr. is a tenured professor of finance and director of the MBA Program at Bowie State University. He has served as a chair of management departments and as a college dean, responsible for six departments representing eight different academic disciplines. He also taught a variety of courses at the graduate and undergraduate levels, from freshman seminar to advanced research classes, in several disciplines including finance, management and economics.

He has successfully coached student teams for national business plan competitions and advised student organizations. He has also developed interdisciplinary curricula with liberal arts colleagues through the *Learning Across the Curriculum* program. His breath and depth of experience resulted in insights about student success in college that he shares with readers in *College in Four Years*.

Dr. Sawyer also developed an externship program, funded by the U.S. Department of Education and in partnership with Addis Abba University in Ethiopia that provided students an opportunity to experience international business, commerce, art and culture on the African continent. He has traveled extensively throughout Asia, Africa, the Americas, the Caribbean and Europe on trade and educational missions.

He has been a speaker at numerous professional meetings, including the Kaufman Foundation Conference on Entrepreneurial Development, the National Association of Investment Companies and the President's Conference on Small Business. He has been published in scholarly journals, including the Journal of Financial Economics and the International Journal of Quality Science. Dr. Sawyer is also a former President of the Board of Education in South Orange-Maplewood, New Jersey.

Dr. Sawyer and his wife, Donna, have two grown daughters and yes, they both graduated college in four years. He is an avid cyclist and on any sunny day, when the temperature is above 55 degrees (and he is not teaching or telling stories at school), you'll find him on the nearest bike trail.

Follow Granville Sawyer on twitter @ProfGMS

ACKNOWLEDGEMENTS

Thank you to all the people who helped me create this book. First, thank you to Donna, my wife, for your support, encouragement and invaluable help. Writing this book would have been impossible without you, and to my children, Jacquelyn and Elizabeth, whose ideas and feedback made this a better book. To my parents, Dr. Granville M. Sawyer, Sr., and Mrs. Maxine Y. Sawyer who showed me the value of education and critical thinking, and Mrs. Millie Lott whose wisdom and insight always kept me going in the right direction. To my editor, Katherine Hamrick, for convincing me I was a writer even when I didn't believe it, and to my students who allowed me to share their experiences and learn from them. To my first readers, Jacquelyn Bullock, Alexis Colander, Millie Lott, Ana Marcano, Molly Matthews, Karen Deans, and Dr. Rod Paige, who gave their time and effort generously to make me a better writer. To Mrs. M. R. Walker, my high school English teacher, who knew what I was really good at before I did.

Contents

INTRODUCTION

CONGRATULATIONS — YOU MADE IT! After months of taking tests, agonizing over applications, waiting for acceptance letters, and wrangling with finances, you're in college.

Every fall, two million eager freshmen enter U.S. colleges and universities. A year after your class enters college, more than one third will not return for the second year. Within six years, only fifty-five percent will graduate with a degree and of those who graduate, only fifty percent of you will end up with jobs after twelve months. If you want to be part of the select group that gets into college, stays and graduates on time with good prospects, then read on.[1,2]

College in Four Years is your plan to ensure that you will be part of the select group that graduates in four years, with excellent prospects. This books gives you a roadmap for how to stay in college, graduate on time and prepare yourself for employment or graduate school.

This book does not tell you how to decorate your dorm room, deal with a roommate, survive dorm or apartment life, join a fraternity or sorority, choose friends, follow fashion, eat, date, party, go on spring break or manage your finances. It is not a mental health handbook. This book offers strategic advice on how to achieve the ultimate objective of your undergraduate education — to earn a degree in four years.

---

[1] http://nces.ed.gov/programs/digest/d12/tables/dt12_376.asp, U.S. Department of Education Institute of Education Sciences National Center for Education Statistics

[2] http://nces.ed.gov/fastfacts/display.asp?id=40, U.S. Department of Education Institute of Education Sciences National Center for Education Statistics

College in Four Years is based on insider knowledge— after working with more than 10,000 students over the course of my thirty-plus years as a professor—I know what it takes to get you *through* college successfully. You won't get this proven information presented this way from counselors, peers, or advisors—most of the advice you've received up to this point is focused on how to get you into college—not how to get you *out*. How do I know the information that I am sharing with you works? I have developed and applied the principles in real time—on campus, in classrooms, in my office, while I'm trying to eat lunch and unfortunately on my way into the men's room—those were particularly short conversations for obvious reasons. I've seen students absorb this information (including my two daughters), use it wisely and succeed in college and beyond. I've also seen students ignore these tactics and fail. I'm hoping that this book will help you to be the former, not the latter.

In short and focused chapters, I make clear points that are concretely supported by informative stories about real students and professors. No sermons or lectures, just sharing stories of experiences with my students and sometimes what I learned the hard way in my own undergraduate and graduate experiences. I also include useful diagrams, tips, worksheets and outlines that enhance this self-driven book. College in four years? Yes! You *can* do it!

PART I

FIRST THINGS FIRST — START WITH THE RIGHT ATTITUDE

CHAPTER I

RUN WITH THE BIG DOGS!

Education is the most powerful weapon which you can use to change the world.

NELSON MANDELA

S TATISTICS SHOW THAT THE DAY you start college, you have just a fifty-five percent chance of finishing in six years and less than a twenty-five percent chance of finishing in four years. This makes every college student a member of a very special group, yet students tend to take this wonderful opportunity for granted and they don't realize, or forget, how special attending college really is. I taught a student who really understood what a special opportunity college was. Ed was back in school after being out for two years. [3,4]

In a candid conversation, he said, "I was seriously injured in a car accident a year and a half ago — so seriously that my heart stopped twice before they finally stabilized me. I ended up needing five surgeries and

3 http://nces.ed.gov/programs/digest/d12/tables/dt12_376.asp, U.S. Department of Education Institute of Education Sciences National Center for Education Statistics
4 http://nces.ed.gov/fastfacts/display.asp?id=40, U.S. Department of Education Institute of Education Sciences National Center for Education Statistics

six months in the hospital before starting physical therapy on a long road to recovery. When I was able to function again, I couldn't wait to get back to school. For a while I didn't think I would be able to finish my degree. I had plenty of time during my rehabilitation to understand how special the chance to go to college was, and this time I wasn't going to take it for granted." He went on to say, "One of the things that's great about college is that you spend time with so many people you have so much in common with. Making friends and starting what can be lifelong relationships is never easier and will never be that easy again." Ed learned how this could be good and bad during his first year in college. The first few weeks on campus were jam-packed, with orientation, schedule planning, classes, new subjects, and activities . . . Most of all, the number and variety of people overwhelmed him.

"I missed my small-town high school, with teachers telling me where to be, what to do, and when to do it," he said. Ed is from the South, with an easy drawl and a memorable way of putting things. "After my accident I had a new appreciation for school and realized that I had a choice. I could either run with the big dogs, doing well in college making good grades, or I could stay on the porch with the puppies, struggling to make C's and D's. I also knew that whatever my choice was, there would be plenty of people to keep me company. At first, I was hanging with the puppies, but that got old fast because A's and F's cost the same thing and I was paying for both! I stepped up and started running with the big dogs and doing what I should have been doing all along—I stopped taking college for granted." Ed told me that there was another reason that he had to run with the big dogs, explaining, "Big dogs eat first."

"What do you mean?" I asked.

"Big dogs eat all the best jobs, the best salaries, and the best of other opportunities in life. The puppies get what's left. I'm not interested in spending the rest of my life eating leftovers. I want to eat first, too!"

THE TAKEAWAY

- Start off with the right attitude about your education, know how special college is. Statistics show that the day you start college, you have less than a fifty-five percent chance of finishing in six years and less than a twenty-five percent chance of finishing in four years.

- Focus on success and understand what a great opportunity this is for you. Remember, it took every day of your life up to yesterday to make today great. It will also take today done well to do tomorrow well. You have no time to waste.

- Run with the big dogs; the big dogs eat first!

CHAPTER 2

TRY OUT A MAJOR BEFORE YOU CHOOSE IT

The things I want to know are in books; my best friend is the man who'll get me a book I ain't read.

ABRAHAM LINCOLN

TRYING TO FIGURE OUT A major in college can be difficult. Before you even get to campus you're asked to choose a major that may set your direction in life for years to come. Not easy!

Joan came to see me totally confused about picking her major — too many choices overwhelmed her.

"I just can't make up my mind," she said. "I don't really understand the catalog descriptions of half the majors." Yet the faculty and guidance counselors kept repeating the same mantra: "Pick a major, pick a major, pick a major." Do it before it's too late, they told her, as if the school would suddenly run out of majors!

"Do not pick your major now, unless you are sure of what you want to do," I advised her. "During the first two years in college, everyone takes

9

the same general education courses; that's by design, to expose you to a number of potential majors *before* you have to decide. Take your time and understand that during the first two years, you can change your major without getting behind or losing any credits."

Joan said that one of the biggest problems with choosing a major was the number of required general education courses.

"You have to take forty three-hour courses for a total of 120 hours to earn a degree. Why so many general education classes? I don't see how they will help me. Each one seems to be another random fifteen-week course—just do the work, get the grade, check off the requirement, and move on to the next one."

"Is this how you plan to deal with every course?" I asked.

"What other way is there?"

"If you follow your current plan, you'll complete your courses one by one, but you won't have a college education," I said. "There is a better way to look at this."

Joan crossed her arms defensively. She didn't want to hear what I had to say, but she needed to hear it.

"Look, life is interdisciplinary," I told her. "You don't have an English part or a math part or a science part. It all comes jumbled together! Part of that jumble will include people who have nothing to do with your major, much less what you do for a living." Joan dropped the attitude and leaned in to follow my big-picture point.

"You need to know something about a lot of different subjects so you can relate to anyone who crosses your path," I said. "Not just one subject and not just your major. That's why you spend a big part of the first two years getting a liberal arts education no matter what major you choose." I further explained that getting her money's worth from college went far beyond her major. She needed to understand how all that extra "stuff" fits together so she could tap into whatever type of knowledge she might need to answer questions or solve problems.

"So you're telling me to be a jack of all trades?" Joan asked.

"That's right. Be a jack of all trades but the master of at least one—your major, when you choose it. Your *mastery* will connect you to your profession. *Knowing something about a lot of different things* will connect you to the rest of the world."

Joan still resisted the concept. "So where does English fit in? We have to read boring essays and short stories and then write about them. Sometimes we have to rewrite a paper multiple times just to get a decent grade."

"Welcome to the real world," I said. "There is no job you'll want that doesn't require excellent writing skills. If you can't write, you can't communicate effectively with anyone. I've seen it over and over again—students who couldn't get or keep a job because of poor writing and/or speaking skills; now they wish they had spent a little more time on those dull English papers. They might have landed the position of their dreams, earned a promotion, or had better opportunities for a job. Let me tell you a story about someone who thought the way you do about all those other courses."

I shared with Joan the story of my friend Richard, who was planning to be an artist, so he didn't worry about anything else. He attended a university where he could study a curriculum highly focused on his major.

"The school kept other areas of study to a minimum," Richard said. "They weren't concerned with anything you might do after graduation except art, so that's all I learned." When Richard graduated, he couldn't find a job as focused as his preparation—positions as art teachers or artists in residence were limited and he was not yet able to earn a living by making and selling his art. With the help of a friend, he ended up taking a job in sales.

Years passed. Richard's financial and personal obligations multiplied, so he stayed in the sales job, always looking for (but never finding) the "exact right job" for him as an artist. He was never happy in sales, despite some success, so he decided to open an art gallery. Richard's art gallery failed.

"The skills I needed were more than just art related," he admitted. "I needed to know how to run a business and how to promote myself. I needed to create a cultural environment for my gallery. I didn't know how to do any of that. The time to learn these things is not when you are launching or running a business."

Richard is now considering going back to school for a business degree. Long before Richard made this admission, I could tell what was troubling him. When we went out with a group of friends, Richard rarely participated in the conversation because discussions regarding art were all he felt he knew enough about to contribute to. Unfortunately for him, that was not a hot topic for the rest of us. We discussed politics, the economy, and other professional and personal endeavors. Richard had nothing to add and even fell asleep a few times when the rest of the group was talking!

A good friend of mine who is a professional recruiter put it this way: "I look for three things when interviewing. Can applicants speak well? Can they write well (proven by an original, well–thought-out cover letter and resume)? Did they come dressed to play—do they know how to dress appropriately for a business environment? If they have these basics down, then we can teach them everything else. If they don't, I'm not interested."

These qualities come from a well-rounded education that has taught you valuable information about a number of disciplines *including* your major. In fact, professionals responding to a survey by the National Association of Colleges and Employers (NACE) said verbal communication skills top the list of "soft" skills they seek in new college graduates.[5]

---

5 http://www.naceweb.org/s10262011/candidate_skills_employer_qualities/, National Association of Colleges and Employers, "Job Outlook: The Candidate Skills/Qualities Employers Want", October 26, 2011.

I told Joan to ask herself the following questions about every course she takes:

- How does this course fit in with others I've taken?

- What about this course do I like?

- What don't I like about this course?

- How does this course fit in with what I'd like to do in the future?

"If you still can't see where this course fits into your plan, ask your professors and advisors the same questions," I told her. "They're a great resource for helping to put your work in context, even when it's not obvious. Understanding the relevance of certain courses and experiences makes choosing a major easier and more meaningful. You'll see how a major fits with what you learn about yourself and about college. And you won't see your general education classes as a bunch of unrelated courses to endure."

A few semesters later, Joan came back to my office eager to tell me about one of the liberal arts courses she had dreaded—a music appreciation course.

"I just took it because I thought it would be a piece of cake," Joan said. "It turned out to be one of the most challenging courses of my college career, and it was unexpected and wonderful. I learned about all kinds of music, and now I've even developed an appreciation for classical music. And, I was even able to use that knowledge to strike up a conversation with an executive who was visiting campus recently. Who knew?"

THE TAKEAWAY

- Taking all those other classes helps you try a major out before you choose it, and, with the right attitude, you'll learn something valuable in every course. It takes more than your major to be successful in work and in life.

- If you wear blinders, you won't see the rest of the world in all its glory and diversity. Knowing a little about a lot increases your desire to learn more and enables you to "hold your own" in any conversation. Plus, it encourages others to respond and express interest in you. Who knows? One may turn into an employer, a client, or someone you'll want to spend more time with!

- Your major might pay the rent every month, but additional accumulated knowledge is critical to gaining specialized skills and connections that give you far more than basic living expenses. You can't make it with just one or the other—you need both.

CHAPTER 3

MAKE SURE THEY KNOW YOU

People will do things you can't ask them to do because they know and like you.

REVEREND FRED D. YOUNG

N O MATTER THE CLASS OR the teachers, make sure they know you. Make sure they can put a face and a person with the name on the roll—believe me, it can make a big difference.

When I was a student, I took an operations research class with a newly minted professor in the business school. Patrick was in his late twenties, with bachelor's and master's degrees in electrical engineering, an MBA, and a PhD in finance—clearly a very smart guy! Well, not quite as smart as I thought.

He spent two weeks of a ten week quarter on a concept in class and then did not include it on the midterm. The class was in shock. We pored over that concept, certain that it would show up prominently on the test.

After we finished the test, a classmate burning with anger said,

"I'm going to see that little **** right now." Fortunately for both of them, Patrick had left campus by the time my friend showed up at his office.

When Patrick handed back the tests, my friend and I received mid-70s scores. Incensed by the poor grade, my friend stood up and was ready to punch Patrick. We sat in the front row, so it wasn't a long walk! I grabbed his shirttail and jerked him back down in his seat.

"If you're that angry, just get your stuff and leave," I said in a low voice. "Leave right now!" He did, slamming the door behind him. Patrick looked at me and asked, "What's wrong with him?"

I played it cool and said, "I have no idea."

Several times during the semester, I had taken the time to see Patrick during his office hours so we could get to know each other. Because of this, I felt comfortable enough to ask him about the test when I went to his office that afternoon.

"I'm not here to talk about my test grade. I could have done better, but what I'm curious about is why you didn't include the concept you spent two weeks going over with us."

"The test had gotten too long by the time I reached the concept so I omitted it," he said.

"You know we were ready for that, don't you?" Patrick agreed that leaving off the subject matter was a mistake.

"I promise that it will be on the final and I will adjust the midterm scores, based on what happened." Because I had developed a relationship with Patrick, I didn't have to ask what "adjust" meant. I was confident he would be fair, and he was. He included the concept on the final and everyone performed much better than on the midterm. I am certain that knowing the work and knowing the professor contributed to earning an A in that class!

THE TAKEAWAY

- Make sure your teachers know you and understand how serious you are about doing well in school. Remind them that you are more than just a name on the roll—that gives your professors an opportunity to respond to you as a person.

- Make a point to see every teacher from every course outside of the classroom at least once during a semester. The biggest chunk of the money you spend on college pays for your instructors, so get your money's worth! Go see them. Let them help you. Make them know who you are!

CHAPTER 4

KNOW THAT SUCCESS IS NOT AUTOMATIC

Intelligence plus character — that is the goal of true education.

MARTIN LUTHER KING JR.

JOAN — THE SAME JOAN who first struggled with all the courses she had to take — became a little more comfortable with the idea of not rushing into a decision (a major) that would affect the rest of her life. She understood the value of taking a variety of courses in the first two years of college to "try out" ideas and experiences to see whether they fit her or not.

I told her, "Each course you take is not just a course. It's your introduction to what could be a job for you in the future or how to build a career."

"Haven't we covered this?" Joan looked ready to leave.

"Not quite," I paused, hoping she would hear me out. "In other words, people *do* for a living what you are studying," I said.

"I never thought about a general education course that way," Joan said.

"Really explore why and how certain courses interest you," I said. "What would it mean if you put into professional practice what you're currently soaking up as facts, theories, problem solving, case studies, and other information?"

"OK, thanks. I'll do that," she said, gathering up her purse and backpack, ready to hit the door.

"Wait," I motioned her to sit down. "There is more to think about."

"OK," she stopped, just to be polite.

"Many students who select their major have no idea what professionals in the field actually do. Instead, be smart, do some research."

"Like what?" she said.

I told her to start with these questions:

- What do people with degrees in this field do?

- What types of jobs are available in this discipline? Are some "hidden" (that is, not as obvious)?

- What are the required skills for the different jobs?

- How much can these professionals advance in their jobs?

- What is the projected growth of available jobs in years to come?

- Where in the world are these jobs?

- Would you want to live in these locations?

- What can you expect to earn at first, and what is the rate of salary increases?

- What are the salaries based on location?

- If you don't want to work for someone else, can you create a job/business in this field as a successful entrepreneur?

- What are the successes and risks for people who own small businesses in this field?

- What does it take to be competitive—GPA, courses, special projects, internships, clubs, and other experiences?

- How will you achieve this competitive profile by graduation?

The questions seemed to pile up for Joan. "I don't have any of that information and I don't know where to get it," she said, knitting her brow in frustration. "And besides . . . that sounds like a lot of work."

"It does take some effort, but you get out of college what you put into it. If you put in the work now, you will reap the benefits later."

"Success is mostly about having good connections and being in the right place at the right time," Joan retorted, "You know, just having a little luck."

Now it was time to turn her thinking around. "So, you think your successful friends who already have jobs owe a lot to luck?"

"Sure, why not?"

"Do you know that what you're saying hurts them *and* you?"

She shrugged.

"Thinking that these people are successful because of luck diminishes all the hard work they put in when you weren't around," I said. "And if you don't work as hard and then don't succeed, you can blame it on your lack of luck. Excuses won't help you. Put in the work now so people will say how 'lucky' you are later. You'll know it's more about hard work than it is about luck, and people who are as successful as you are will know it too."

"Even if I'm willing to do the work, where do I get all that information to get started?"

I gave Joan another list so she could start to build a network and look for opportunities in and out of school.

- Start with your teachers. Ask about professionals in your field. Find out what they do. Do your teachers know someone who would be willing to meet with you for an informational interview, to talk to you about their work and share ideas to inform and inspire your professional plans?

- Go to the career services/placement office for information on the field that interests you. Also, ask about relevant internships, even if you aren't ready right now.

- Go to career fairs, even if you won't graduate for a couple of years—you can't start too soon. Talk to the company recruiters in your field. Get to know them. Get their business cards and keep track of them. You will not have a lot of time with them, so prepare to tell them about yourself in a concise manner (one minute or less) so you can spend the rest of your time soaking up relevant information. Ask if you can contact them in the future, and hopefully they will help you connect with others in their companies. Take all their handouts and social networking URLs. Check out their company videos on YouTube. Make sure they know you and you know them.

- If there is a college chapter of a professional organization related to your field, join and actively participate. Go to every meeting and activity sponsored by your chapter. Be willing to serve on committees and as an officer. Join the committee that seeks out professional speakers. Network with every speaker. One example of such an organization is the student arm of the American Marketing Association. They offer students internship resources, job boards, information about graduate school, and additional opportunities.

- Tell your teachers and department chair about your memberships and activities. When potential employers ask them—or the dean of your school—about good students, they will always think of you.

- Hang around! With the right people that is. This is networking, too. If you don't have to, don't rush out of the building when class is over. Talk to friends and classmates or drop in on a favorite teacher. Make sure they know your name. When something good comes along or one of your classmates finds out something important, such as a career connection or a job opportunity, you'll be the one they seek out.

- Be ready! You never know when or where you'll run into someone who has an opportunity for you. Come to school dressed as who you would like to be, not somebody who just rolled out of bed and threw on yesterday's wrinkled clothes. This doesn't mean wearing a suit or dress every day—less than fifteen percent of jobs today require that. However, it does mean dressing neatly, being well-groomed, and staying organized. It means being ready to promote yourself and what you want to do at any time. This includes keeping an up-to-date resume with you at all times; however, don't force it on a professional, but be ready if they ask for it. It also means staying current on major corporate and industry news for the places/companies you hope to work for one day.

- Attend networking events in the community—mentors and professors can help you locate them. If you happen to meet a professional, be ready, if they show interest. After a quick introduction, ask about their company and their job. They may say, "So tell me about yourself." This is the number one "make or break" question in a job interview. You have 30 to 60 seconds to grab and keep their attention—it's called an elevator speech. Some people glaze over after 30 seconds. You need a hook and a story-like summary—make yourself memorable!

"So I need to look serious about what I'm doing and have my elevator speech ready at all times," Joan asked.

"Yes, absolutely," I replied. "So what would be your elevator speech?"

"I should be ready to talk about my educational accomplishments and the type of position I'm looking for, based on my qualifications," Joan said quickly.

I said, "That sounds good, but emphasize what you can *do* and less about abstract descriptions of yourself. In other words, what questions can you answer and what problems can you solve for the person you're talking to."

"Suppose I don't know much about the person or the company?" Joan asked. "I won't know specific questions or problems they have."

I said, "That's an excellent point. If you jump in and talk too fast and too much about yourself, you'll lose control of the conversation."

"I don't understand," Joan said. "If you're talking, aren't you controlling what's being discussed and when?"

I shook my head. "That isn't the way you want to do it. After your elevator speech breaks the ice, wait for the expert to talk. You can't get key information if you're talking nonstop."

"You're right," Joan said. "It's so annoying to talk to people who go on and on about themselves."

I smiled. "That's right. Listen first, then talk—not the other way around. That gives you an opening to ask more questions about the person, their company, and the challenges and opportunities the company is facing in the marketplace. Keep in mind that it's about them, not about you. Then use what you just learned to present yourself in the most appealing way that is relevant to their situation."

"That's what my speech teacher said: show, don't tell," said Joan.

"That's it! Keep it short and focused. Be yourself—no fancy words."

"OK, the clock is ticking. How do I finish before this person walks off?"

"Don't let the conversation dribble off. Keep control and wrap it up. Express your thanks and ask for a business card and an opportunity to follow up once you have taken more courses in your major."

"Is there anything else I should do?" asked Joan.

"If you *really* feel comfortable with this person, ask for a fifteen-minute informational interview for additional career and industry advice. Use the research questions we talked about earlier—on how to ask professionals about their field. Don't come off as if you're asking for a job interview. If you ask the right way, most people are happy to schedule some time."

"That's a lot to think about," Joan said. "I'd better get started so I'll stand out the way I want to."

"That's right, get going. In a way, you're competing with every student who has that professional's attention . . . and one more thing."

"What?"

"Send a thank-you note within twenty-four hours! An e-mail is fine. But here's a secret: at least fifty percent of executives prefer a hand-written note, and it will make you stand out."

"Thanks!" Joan zipped out of my office. Her thank-you note appeared in my inbox the next day.

THE TAKEAWAY

- Use the tips in this chapter and do your research. You'll be amazed at how "lucky" you can be when you put them to work. Remember, success in college and afterward is not automatic today or in the future.

FOLLOW-UP EXERCISE

Interview your mentors, teachers, advisors, and the professionals they recommend, using the *Career Research Questionnaire* on the next page.

Career Research Questionnaire

This set of questions will help you research prospective fields that interest you. Ask your mentors, teachers, advisors, and other professionals they recommend.

1. What do people with degrees in this field do?

2. What is the variety of jobs? Are some "hidden" (that is, not as obvious)?

3. What are the required skills?

4. How much can these professionals advance in their jobs?

5. What is the projected growth of available jobs in years to come?

6. Where in the world are these jobs?

7. Would you want to live in these locations?

8. What can you expect to earn at first and what are the rates of salary increases? Are salaries based on location? If so, ask for more details.

9. If you don't want to work for someone else, can you create a job/business in this field as a successful entrepreneur?

10. What are the successes and risks to owning a small business in this field?

11. What does it take to be competitive — GPA, courses, special projects, internships, clubs, and other experiences?

12. How will you achieve this competitive profile by graduation?

CHAPTER 5

Don't Pay to Fail

Children must be taught how to think, not what to think.

Margaret Mead

Sometimes it's hard to make people understand what going to college is really like—*for you*. Your parents, friends, family, classmates, and colleagues may be able to empathize or sympathize, but you are the only one who can really know your experience.

Rob, a student in one of my classes, wasn't doing well. He attended every class but just didn't seem to be able to handle the work. His grades kept slipping.

One day I asked him, "Do you need tutoring, help with test preparation, or something else?"

"No, I'm OK," Rob said. "I'll catch up and do better."

"That's what you want to do, but what *can* you do?" I asked.

"I have to pass this class," he said desperately. "I need to keep going and keep up my GPA."

Rob was in trouble, someone was clearly pressuring him, but he didn't share who or why so I couldn't help him. Rob failed my class, his grade wasn't even close to passing. A few days after I turned in my grades, I saw Rob.

"Thanks for the F!" he said and shook my hand with gratitude. I don't usually get that kind of response for that kind of grade, so I was a little shocked and just said, "You're welcome!"

Rob explained, "My father had been pressuring me to be active in the fraternity that he pledged when he was going to this school. He stayed on my case to do this while keeping a B+ GPA majoring in finance and playing the same sports he did. This was too much for me, but he just wouldn't listen."

Now I started to understand.

"My father would say, 'Work a little harder. Bear down. You can do it; I did!'"

Rob said his relationship with his father worsened. "We talked less and less because every conversation ended in the same argument."

In the end, Rob's father got the message. "The F—the first failing grade I ever earned—finally convinced my father that he was asking too much of me," Rob said.

Don't wait for failing grades to teach you the lesson Rob and his father learned. Make sure you're honest with yourself about how much you can really take on and do well while you are in college. Can you work thirty hours every week *and* go to school full-time *and* make the dean's list? Don't be afraid to share that information and your concerns with anyone who can assist you, whether or not a parent or someone else may be confusing their college career with yours. Give your professors as much information as possible so they can help you succeed.

There will be many opportunities and activities inside and outside the classroom—more than you can possibly manage. There will always be someone to invite—or tempt—you to lose sight of your priorities. Put school and *your* objectives first. The fun you had with your friends and the money you made working a part- or full-time job will just be memories when you graduate. However, your academic performance will follow you for years.

THE TAKEAWAY

- Nobody is going to ask about how much fun you had in college or care how many friends you had. They won't ask how much money you made on jobs to support yourself unless those jobs are related to your degree and make you better qualified for a position.

- Many people — the ones important to your future — will ask what you studied and how well you did. What's more, they will make pivotal decisions that affect your future, including job offers, based on your answers.

- Doing well in school is what's most important. Don't let anyone convince you otherwise.

CHAPTER 6

IF THEY ASK YOU TO LIE, CHEAT, OR STEAL — DON'T!

To educate a person in the mind but not in morals is to educate a menace to society.

THEODORE ROOSEVELT

ONNA, A COLLEAGUE OF MINE, is a very talented and creative person. As long as the work is creative, she excels in her field of marketing and public relations. However, she's always struggled with quantitative material. One of the courses she was required to take and pass for her MBA was a computer science class that required each student to write a computer program. Donna said, "The assignment was very challenging, and everyone in the class was struggling to get the program right, especially me. As the due date for the program approached, a classmate asked me if I wanted to chip in on the cost of hiring a professional programmer to write the program that they would all turn in. Even though I was struggling, I said no thanks."

When Donna got to this point in the story, I really hoped that "justice was done." I didn't want the students to benefit from cheating, but I also hoped Donna didn't end up failing the class because she didn't cheat. I wasn't disappointed. Donna said, "The instructor saw that all the other students' programs were exactly alike, so he knew right away that they had cheated. The only program that was different was mine. It wasn't completely right, but it was my work. I ended up being the only student who passed the course! While I'm still not fond of quantitative material, putting in the time and effort to get that program right boosted my confidence and confirmed that my ethics were in the right place."

THE TAKEAWAY

- Don't cut corners to get through college; you'll only hurt yourself.

- In addition to not gaining the knowledge you would have if you didn't cut corners, you're also sending a strong message to anyone who knows what you did. One seemingly small decision can make people assume that you will lie, cheat, or steal to get what you want, in any situation. And make no mistake about it, someone will know, and they are going to make decisions about you as a person, based on what they know.

- If anyone asks you to lie, cheat, steal, or do anything you're uncomfortable with, don't do it! Don't convince yourself that what you are going to do is "really not that wrong or bad" so it's OK. It isn't!

CHAPTER 7

MAKE YOUR OWN LUCK, THEN MAKE YOUR LIFESTYLE

Often, it's not about becoming a new person,
but becoming the person you were meant
to be, and already are, but don't know how
to be.

HEATH L. BUCKMASTER, BOX OF HAIR: A FAIRY TALE

ONE OF THE BIGGEST CHALLENGES you'll face in college is staying focused on what matters. Joe wandered into my office one day by mistake; he was looking for the professor next door. When I told him that, he said, "Well, since I'm here, tell me about the MBA program—I'm graduating this semester and might be interested."

Joe was finishing his degree in information systems but was not satisfied with the response he was getting from potential employers. He was getting interviews but no job offers. "This makes no sense to me because I know more than most people in my classes, including the teachers," he said, quite sure of himself.

"So you're smart, get excellent grades, and you're not getting job offers," I said. That's when he told me his grade point average was 2.54.

"Joe, that's not going to get you the attention you want—especially the kind of attention you're looking for from employers," I told him. "Employers consider your grade point average when they're deciding who to hire. There really isn't much you can do about your GPA now; however, there is something else you can do."

"What?" he said as if he'd heard it all before (remember he told me that he was smarter than most people in his classes).

"Go to graduate school. Get an MBA and get a 3.54 GPA in the process. When hiring managers see that you did well in graduate school, they won't ask about your undergraduate GPA. Your current GPA might be good enough to get you into an accredited MBA program, so think seriously about this."

"That sounds fine," Joe said, "but I don't have the money to go to graduate school."

"Do you have any school loans to pay off or other financial obligations after graduation?" I asked.

"Not really, my parents helped pay for my tuition, but they said graduate school would be on me," he shrugged. "I have a job now and could probably support myself and pay for graduate school, except there are other priorities." I asked Joe about his job. He told me he was a Pepsi distributor.

"That sounds great," I said. "How large is your territory? How many people work for you? What kind of future prospects do you have?"

"No, you don't understand what I'm saying," Joe said. "I drive a delivery truck distributing Pepsi to my assigned stores. I've been doing this for the last two years of college, as a part-time job that helped me through, but it's not something I can make a career of."

"Fine," I said. "Keep the job, borrow what you need, and get your MBA."

"I don't know," said Joe. "I have still have issues to consider."

"Like what?" I couldn't wait to hear what issues he might have.

"You see, I have a lifestyle to maintain," Joe said. "If I went to graduate school, I would have to make big changes."

"What do you mean?"

Joe said that he and his girlfriend vacationed and entertained with friends. "I can't sacrifice any of this for graduate school because, after all, we have a lifestyle that we really enjoy."

I asked Joe how he planned to keep living that way after graduation, since he would no longer be on his parents' payroll and his job prospects didn't look too bright. I asked him whether he could stay on at Pepsi.

"No, I've talked with them about a full-time position, but they said they're not hiring right now. Still, I'm not worried," he said blithely. "All I need to do is meet some people who are smart enough to see my skills and talents. They'll hire me."

Joe had all the answers, but they weren't the right ones and he wasn't ready for reality yet, so at that point, all I could say was, "Joe, it was nice talking to you. Good luck with your life and your lifestyle!"

THE TAKEAWAY

- Don't get distracted by a "lifestyle" that depends on resources you don't have or that are about to run out. Lifestyle can wait.

- Focus on your education now so you'll have everything you'll need to live the way you desire. That's when people, including Joe, will look at you and say, "Aren't you lucky." But you'll know otherwise. You were smart enough to earn it!

PART II

GET THE RIGHT ADVICE
AT THE RIGHT TIME

CHAPTER 8

TAKE THE RIGHT CLASS AT THE RIGHT TIME

The facts are always friendly, every bit of evidence one can acquire, in any area, leads one that much closer to what is true.

CARL ROGERS

M Y NEIGHBOR'S SON, JORDAN, IS going to college soon, and since I work at a university, he wanted to know how to choose classes.

"My brother is in college now, listening to him decide which classes he should take confused me," Jordan said.

"For your first semester, someone will advise you on which classes you should take," I told him. "After that, you'll talk with your advisor each semester, but you will be responsible for making the final decision."

"So that means I should take the classes my advisor says I should take?"

"Not quite," I said. "Each semester you'll need to work *with* your advisor to make decisions together. Never assume you can just do what someone else says. Always think and decide for yourself."

This process becomes more complicated as students move more deeply into their majors. For example, all business majors at my university take the same advanced management course as one of the last courses they need to graduate, no matter what their major is. This course requires them to have already taken and passed a mathematics course, macro and microeconomics, two accounting courses, Principles of Management, Principles of Finance, and two business law courses, whew! Students can't take the economics courses until they've taken the math course. They can't take the accounting courses until they've taken the math course, plus another math course that prepares them for the accounting courses, and they can't take the accounting courses simultaneously. And, they can't take the Principles of Finance course until they have taken and passed all of the previously mentioned math and accounting courses! When you lay out all of this on a timeline, it takes four semesters of course planning to be ready to take that last management course! So a student needs to start thinking about and planning to take their final advanced management course at least four semesters before they take it—as soon as they begin taking business courses.

"Some students do this right and some don't," I told Jordan. "For example, I got a call from Frieda, a student who needed permission to take the advanced management course, because she didn't have all the prerequisites (the courses she had to complete before taking the management course). It turns out that she had not taken Principles of Finance or the second accounting course required for Principles of Finance, so she didn't even have the prerequisite for the prerequisite! I asked her what would happen if she didn't take the management course that semester. She said she wouldn't graduate on time."

I said, "I'm afraid you're going graduate later than you planned, because it would take *at least* three semesters to finish. The accounting course must be taken and passed *before* finance, which must be taken and passed *before* the management course."

"That sounds really complicated," said Jordan, shaking his head.

"Here's the secret, Jordan," I said. "You have to know when to take the courses you need so you can take the *right* course at the *right* time. You can use semester-by-semester class schedules from the school catalog or from your department or your academic advisor to learn this important information."

I went on to explain that students should not take classes that are convenient because they want to sleep in or go to class only two days a week. Let me repeat this, because it is critical — **students should not take classes that are convenient because they want to go to class only two days a week or because they don't want early classes or some other convenience-based reason.** You need to understand what prerequisites you need *before* — not during or after — the semester starts.

"That's what I mean when I say you need to think and decide for yourself," I said. "When you go to college, your advisors and professors will expect that you know how to do this, because the information on prerequisites is easy to find in the college catalog. You'll make college a lot easier if you understand this."

"That makes sense," said Jordan, "I'll remember to check my prerequisites every time I'm choosing my classes."

The Takeaway

- In college, there will be a number of prerequisites that determine the order of classes to be taken. Be like Jordan — learn about them ahead of time and plan. Never delay!

Follow-up Exercise

If you want to graduate in four years, you must closely track the order in which you must take required courses for your major. For an example, see the following *Map Your Courses: Class Sequence Diagram*. Use this model to create your own course-tracking diagram. Show it to your advisor when you review your schedule and update it as you move through your courses.

Map Your Courses: Sample Class Sequence Diagram

You plan is to graduate in four years, right? Then take control of mapping your courses the minute you declare a major. Talk to your advisor at every step (you may want to check out the process when you are researching a possible major). The diagram on the following page is how a business student would map out required courses. Create your own diagram to guide you, based on your major, information you get from your advisor, and your school's course catalog.

Missing a prerequisite could force you to take an additional semester or two! Do you really want to spend that additional time and money?

Sample Class Sequence Diagram

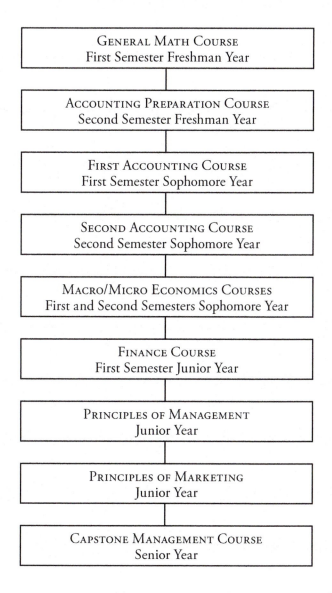

CHAPTER 9

It's All Up to Your Advisor, Right?

I learned in an extremely hard way that the accountability falls with me.

Stephen Baldwin

I CONSIDER ACADEMIC ADVISING TO BE one of my most important responsibilities. It is where I can make a real difference in a student's college experience, but only if they meet me halfway.

Brittany swooped into my office one day as if she were late to an important meeting. She said what she wanted would only take a couple of minutes. She just needed me to approve the last five courses she needed to graduate.

"I know what I need to take, so you just have to check off my courses, and I will be on my way," she said breathlessly.

"Brittany, slow down a bit so I can know what you know," I said. She was still impatient, but she waited.

"Did you check your degree progress report that shows all courses taken and what's left before you graduate?"

"Yes, I've done that."

"When?" Brittany hesitated and then admitted she last looked at the report about two years ago.

"Let's check again, just to be sure," I said, insisting that we comb through it in detail. "Well," I finally said, "it looks like you have ten courses left, not five."

Brittany sat in stunned silence. Now she had two semesters to pay for and finish, not one.

"This report was available at any time," I said. "Why didn't you look at it?"

"I thought everything was OK." Brittany said looking down. That was all she could say, and she left my office in shock. After Brittany's shock wore off, she returned to my office, ready for action. Together, we developed a plan that would enable her to finish college in two semesters. Brittany believed she could advise herself, and it cost her an extra semester in school.

Another student, John, had a different approach. John dropped by, confused about how he should proceed in planning his classes. He didn't seem too worried; he merely looked at me and said, "So, tell me what classes to take."

John came empty handed, without a pen, notebook, nor a scrap of paper, clearly expecting me to do all the work.

I looked at him and his cavalier attitude and firmly said, "That's not what I'm here to do. I advise you; I don't tell you what to do."

"If you're not going to tell me what to take, who will?" John asked.

"No one will," I said and then told him how to prepare for our next meeting by looking at his degree progress report so he would know what he had taken and gotten credit for and what classes he had left to take. Then he needed to select courses for the next semester and bring the list to our next meeting for approval.

"Don't come back until you've completed everything asked of you," I cautioned.

I saw John about two weeks later. He was a different person: prepared, thoughtful, and fully aware of his academic situation. He answered all my questions about the courses he needed to take and whether he was ready to take them, and we finished in about fifteen minutes. From that moment, until he graduated, John took control of his education, needing only minimal guidance from me.

THE TAKEAWAY

Answer these questions and you will be on your way to taking control of your undergraduate education!

- See your advisor and get the information you need to take control of your college experience. If the advisor you are assigned isn't helping you, ask to be assigned to someone who can. Don't go without the information you will need.

- Are you planning and periodically [double] checking all the courses necessary to graduate? It's fine to take other courses along the way, but don't get careless about the ones you absolutely need to get your degree.

- Have you completed all prerequisite courses *before* the courses that require them? I see students on a regular basis who beg me to get them into courses they don't meet the prerequisites for to graduate. I can't do that and no other academic professional will either—it violates university policy.

- Will all your required courses be available when you need to take them? Don't reach your last year and find out you need to take a fall course in the spring and a spring course in the fall. Courses in your major may even alternate annually. Check the current catalog—it's online insurance at your fingertips.

- What other requirements are there for graduation? For example, certain courses may demand grades at a certain level — and nothing lower. Others may stipulate certain restrictions regarding where you must take your final hours. Some universities require that undergraduates take their last thirty hours on campus.

- Do you know the clearance process for graduation and what you will need to do and when? If you must fill out and turn in forms and/or pay a fee by a certain deadline, do it. Don't be late!

- Know that the catalog you are admitted under is like a contract between you and the university. It clearly specifies all the conditions for graduation and is your assurance that the courses will be offered, as shown in the catalog, so they can be taken in the right sequence to graduate in four years. Every institution of higher education must have clearly stated policies about changing the catalog you are under, located in the catalog itself.

Answer these questions at least four semesters before graduation, not four weeks before you expect to march.

CHAPTER 10

WHAT TO DO TODAY
AND TOMORROW

Education is our passport to the future, for tomorrow belongs to the people who prepare for it today.

MALCOLM X

ALICIA, A STUDENT IN THE business college, came by to see me with questions about the career day the college recently hosted. "I talked with some successful people and listened to their presentations, but they didn't help me a lot," she said. "They all seemed to say the same thing. 'This is who I am, this is what I do, and if you work hard, you can do it too.'"

"That sounds OK to me," I said. "What's wrong with that advice?"

"That doesn't help me today," Alicia said, "I wanted them to help me with what I need to do *now* to get where they are. I know doing well in school is important, but I know there's more. I'm sure they had classmates who were good students but did not succeed at the same level. What made the difference? Right now, I don't see how to get from where I am to where they are. They didn't explain that part very well, and that's the most important part to me."

"Did you ask the speakers, 'What's the next step for me? What can I do now, aside from doing well in school?'"

"Not really," she said. "Nobody told me how to do that. Besides, none of the other students were asking those questions." I told Alicia to speak up next time because the people talking to her have the answers, if she asks the right questions. I gave her examples of some questions to ask:

- Did you have a plan for success after college?

- If you did, what was it?

- Did it work?

- If it did, why did it work?

- How much of what you did can I use today?

- What do you think I need to do in the current business environment?

- Will you help me make my plan as you did?

"This is how these professionals can be most helpful to you now and in the future," I said. "You can use the answers you get to those questions to determine long-range and short-range goals, using the statements below." In other words, in order to complete immediate tasks every semester, she needed to set goals on a yearly basis, while addressing shorter time frames—six months, three months, one month one week, etc. . . .

- **In five years, I want to have a position or start a business in** _____. This is an answer experienced people can help with most because they are where she wants to be in five or more years.

- **In four years, I want to** _____. "This is when answers to the previous questions can be useful," I told Alicia. "When you have an idea of what goals you need to achieve and by when, you can complete this statement. This and all the other annual goals are the ones your mentors — the people who are coaching you — can help answer. This is also when your college career plan kicks in, because you may be four years away from graduation."

- **In three years, I want to _____.** This is closer to where you are now — career day. Ask your mentors specifically about what they did or didn't do in college to help them accomplish their plan. Ask for advice about what you should or shouldn't do.

- **In two years, I want to _____.** "This should be the time you make a final decision on a major," I said. "Don't rely only on your personal experience, good or bad. You need to talk to your mentors, teachers, and advisors about this choice. They can help, but they are not mind readers. Just ask.

- **In one year, I want to _____.** "Based on the two-, three-, and four-year goals you've already set, you should have some idea of what you need to do the next year," I told Alicia. "This includes courses to take and other activities, such as internships and participation in professionally related groups. Keep working with your mentors, teachers, and advisor, because they are the most valuable resources you have.

- **In six months, I want to _____.** I spelled out the details that Alicia should outline every semester. Now you should identify this clearly, so you can follow the strategy you've laid out. Keep your advisory "team" informed of your progress. The minute you have a question, ask for guidance. Calculate the grades you need in classes you are taking this semester and next to get/keep your grade point average where it needs to be. See your instructor(s) about your calculations if you have questions and to confirm your calculations. I've provided a worksheet in **Chapter 16** to calculate projected grades, based on estimates of scores on tests yet to be taken in the current semester. Follow up with any professional contacts you've made, to further develop relationships that can lead to internships and/or jobs after graduation.

- **In three months, I want to** _____.
  With the three-month plan, evaluate expectations for the semester. Update your performance calculations to ensure you are still on track for your desired grades. If you need help in classes, get it now! Allow enough time to prepare for tests and turn in assignments on time. Start planning for assignments and projects that are due at the end of the semester; students trap themselves into last minute all-nighters too often and for no reason. Don't wait until the end of the semester to ask for extra credit.

- **In one month, I want to** _____.
  Check off end-of-semester details. Collect the resources you need, schedule study time, and meet with instructors to verify what you need to do to close out the semester. You need to think about administrative tasks; don't let them sneak up on you! Check those prerequisites and required courses on your progress report. Pre-register early on for courses next semester, including the all-important ones that fill up fast.

- **In one week, I want to** _____.
  Weeks can fly by, sometimes in a blur. Break down each week so your monthly goals stay on track.

- **Tomorrow I will** _____.
  Base tomorrow's goals on what has to be done this week. Enter the details in your calendar, even if they seem insignificant. Even short obligations can eat into your day, and they may distract you from more important activities. Account for the hours. Use the blank format at **www.GranvilleSawyer.com/resources** to complete the Key Questions: What is my Plan to Succeed in College.

THE TAKEAWAY

- I've heard students resist developing a plan, saying, "This sounds really good, but I don't have time to do it." My answer is always the same: "You'll be surprised at how much time you have when you plan well. Don't convince yourself it can't be done."

- Have confidence in yourself and your professors. Ask for help and let us work with you. Success will never be an accident. It will only come because you envisioned and followed a plan.

Go to **www.granvillesawyer.com/resources/** to get your own interview and planning sheets with the questions from this chapter. Click on "Ask The Professionals: What Was Your Post-College Plan For Success?" and "Key Questions: What Is My Plan To Succeed In College?" Examples of what can be found on the web site appear in the Appendix.

PART III

How to Use the Resources You Have

CHAPTER 11

Use Your Textbook
the Right Way

Anyone who stops learning is old, whether at twenty or eighty. Anyone who keeps learning stays young.

HENRY FORD

RICHARD TOOK MY PRINCIPLES OF Finance course. He came to every class, was attentive, and took notes. He lacked just one thing—a book.

When I asked him about it, he said, "The book's just too expensive. It costs almost $200!"

I looked down at his feet and asked, "How much did that brand new pair of designer shoes cost?" His response, "I can't remember."

"I know the book is expensive, but you can't pass the class without it," I said. "The concepts I expect you to understand are explained in the book. Your homework problems are from the book. Class notes aren't enough. You need the book to understand the details of what I cover in class."

"I know . . . you're right," Richard acknowledged. "I'll get the book right away." He didn't, and he failed Principles of Finance.

Anthony, who was in the same class as Richard, couldn't afford the books either, so he bought them used, shared books, or made other arrangements to use the textbook(s) when necessary.

"I knew I had to have the book because this is a numbers class," he said. I looked at his book and noticed that it was well worn. "It sure looks like you've been using that book," I said.

"Well, it was used when I got it, but I've been reading it a lot, so it's a lot more used now. I study the book because that's where the knowledge is!" Anthony said. "Everything I want to know about the stuff in this class is in there. I just have to pull it out."

"Do you read the book to understand what we go over in class?"

"At first, I do, but that's not enough for me," he said. "Reading isn't understanding; it's just reading. That's why, after reading some of a chapter, I close the book and try to write a summary of what I just read," he said. "If I can't, it means I either don't remember or don't understand or both — that means I have to go back and read again. The summary is my test of understanding. This strategy takes a lot longer to get through the chapter — sometimes two or three times as long — but at the end, I understand it and I have written proof. Or at least I know what questions to ask you in class."

"I also use an outline of the chapter as a tool to study for tests," he said. "So I don't have to go back and reread everything." Anthony's system caught my attention because it worked; he was an excellent student.

I asked, "Does your system help you work out the problems, since they are numeric and most of the chapter isn't?"

"When I started using my system," Anthony explained, "I really didn't know why it worked — it just did. After a while, I realized that my system helped me solve every type of problem I came across." It was clear that Anthony's critical thinking had kicked in, with the help of his system.

"This came from understanding the words and the examples," he continued. "When I was just picking through the chapter to find the right formula to get the right answer, I couldn't see this. So on tests, I couldn't recognize a type of problem when I saw it again, even though I had done at least one just like it in the homework. If you can't figure out what kind of problem it is, you can't work it!"

THE TAKEAWAY

- Anthony's system helped him recognize what was important about each chapter, even in "numbers" classes. Everything the textbook author talks about applies consistently to all problems of a certain type. If you understand the content in the textbook, you will understand how all of the problems of this type work and how to recognize them when you see them again — like maybe on a test. That will make you a numbers superstar, instead of a "mechanic." Mechanics know how to manipulate numbers and formulas to get answers for specific problems they do, but they don't know why they're doing it. Because of this, the next time they see a problem that is similar, but not exactly the same as the one they did, they don't know how to do it.

- There won't be an easy "recipe" for the tests encountered in school or in life. No one will tell you what to do — no simple cookbook!

  o "A" students know how and why.

  o "B" students know how and a lot of why.

  o "C" students know how and some why.

  o "D" students know some of how and very little of why.

  o "F" students have no clue about how or why!

- Be an "A" student—see if Anthony's summary, outline, and review system works for you to learn the how and the why of what you study. If his system doesn't work—figure out why and create your own system!

CHAPTER 12

READ THE TEXTBOOK BEFORE CLASS

If you don't have time to do it right, when will you have time to do it over?

JOHN WOODEN

FOR EVERY COURSE YOU TAKE, the instructor should hand you a syllabus on your first day of class. The syllabus lays out your semester like a roadmap and shows what the instructor will cover and what he or she expects from you. Hang on to it! The syllabus should specifically detail:

- What the professor plans to cover during the semester
- When tests/homework/presentations/other projects are due and/ or scheduled
- How you'll be graded on the work that you do
- How that work will count toward your final grade
- How the professor will calculate the final grade

- How the number grade corresponds to the letter grade in the course

The syllabus will also show what you should read prior to every class meeting, and if you want to ensure that you complete college in four years, read the assigned material before class! Don't hear about information for the first time from your teacher in class. Here's a story about what can happen if you don't go to class prepared.

One day I watched my students busily taking notes on what I was saying and the information I wrote on the board. I decided to try a little experiment. I kept talking but started giving them obviously erroneous information about our discussion topic. To make things a bit more interesting, I put the incorrect information on the board. I figured someone would call me on it and say, "Isn't that wrong?" No one did; they kept writing, not missing a word.

After a few minutes, I stopped and showed the students what I had done. They were more annoyed about having to change their notes than the fact that I gave them incorrect information.

When class ended a student asked me why I put wrong information on the board. "We trust you to give us the right information," she said. "You shouldn't play tricks on us like that."

"Did you know the information was wrong?" I asked.

"Of course not," she said. "We're supposed to *trust* you."

"In other words, you don't think about what you're writing; you just write it down."

"Isn't that what I'm supposed to do? I read my notes later to understand the material you covered in class."

"Have you ever taken notes that you didn't understand or seemed incomplete?" I asked.

"Sure."

"OK, here's the idea," I said. "Understand what you're writing now so it makes sense later. Ask the questions when they pop into your head. If you wait until the next class to ask, the information is going to pile up on top of the new information. You're going to be one class behind all the time."

"But there's no time for that in class," Joy said. "There's too much to do."

"I agree with you," I said. She looked surprised; she had not expected that response.

"Let's make a short list of all the things you tried to do simultaneously in class," I said. It included:

- Listen to me.

- Look at and understand what I write on the board.

- Take notes that you can read and understand after class; write clearly so you won't waste time later trying to decipher a bunch of scrawls or misspelled gibberish.

- Look at the book and understand what is in there, even if for the first time.

- Ask questions about the discussed material, whether you go back to the book, talk to your classmates, or review it with your professor during an office visit.

"How many of these did you achieve today?" I asked Joy.

"Almost all of them," she said and then hesitated. "Well, at least three or four."

"Really, which three or four?" Joy looked at the list and couldn't decide. So I said, "You didn't do any of them well because you were trying to do all of them at the same time. Nobody can do that. You're trying to do so many things that you don't have time to think."

"But all those things have to be done," insisted Joan. "I can't take any of them off the list."

"I agree with you, but do they all have to be done in class?" I asked. "One of the biggest differences between 'A' students and everyone else is that *they read the book before class*." I explained to Joy that there is no substitute for reading the book before class and there are several great advantages:

- You know what you understand and what you don't understand.

- You know what questions to ask before class starts.

- You recognize when the teacher is reviewing familiar material.

- The notes you take make more sense because you've seen the information before.

- You can concentrate on taking clear notes when the teacher explains something you don't understand.

- You won't complain that your professor is "going too fast." You'll know how and when to stop him or her.

When you read the material to be covered beforehand, class will seem easier—like taking cool sips of water rather than trying to gulp from a fire hose. Joy started reading her textbook. She came prepared for class; I could tell that by the questions that she asked and the answers that she gave. She came by my office the next semester to confirm what I saw.

"Reading ahead of time made a big difference," she said. "I knew the material better and I did better in class. Now I tell all my friends, if you want to do well and save time in the long run, read the book *before* class!"

THE TAKEAWAY

- Read the assigned material in your textbook, as detailed in your syllabus, before class. Write down questions as you read so you can ask them in class. Be determined to get an answer you understand. If you don't, go see your teacher after class.

- Working hard in college is not enough. You can work your butt off and still fail. People do it every day. You have to work hard and work smart to be successful in college. You can't make it with just one. Now, open that textbook before class!

CHAPTER 13

You Can't Study with a Study Group

Teamwork is so important that it is virtually impossible for you to reach the heights of your capabilities or make the money that you want without becoming very good at it.

BRIAN TRACY

I stopped Dr. Jones, who teaches freshman seminar classes, in the hall to ask about a discussion topic.

"What about doing a seminar on creating and using study groups?" I asked.

"That's a definite possibility," she said.

"Students need to understand that you can't study with a group." Dr. Jones took a step back.

"What do you mean? Isn't that what study groups are for?"

"I don't think so," I replied. "Let me tell you about a group of students I'm dealing with now. Seven students formed a study group and, according to them, did everything they were supposed to do. They divvied up taking notes and making outlines from class. They met regularly and used the group notes to study for exams. They all failed the class."

Dr. Jones was dumbfounded. "Why?" she asked.

"After talking extensively with all of them as a group as well as individually, I figured out what happened," I said. "I told all of them that the best way to study, actually learn, and assimilate information is *alone*."

Dr. Jones smiled. "They didn't believe you."

"Not a word."

Then I explained to Dr. Jones how I shared a few simple points with my students:

- You can't count on using the notes taken by others. The person that took those notes learned, assimilated information, and made notes best suited to *their* learning style, not yours.

- Your learning process did not kick in, no matter how carefully you read their notes. Why? Because you didn't put in the time on those notes; they did.

- The only material you've mastered is based on the notes you make — on your time.

"This group still didn't believe me," I said, "so I set up an experiment." I walked Dr. Jones through my little exercise in which I asked the students to bring me their group notes for the course, with each set identified by the student who made them. Then I set up the ground rules: I would ask the group questions; however, the student who took the related notes could not answer. For the most part, the students did not know or only partially knew answers from notes made by their counterparts. They were surprised.

"We read through every set of notes," they said. "We were sure we knew the material." These folks found out the hard way that group knowledge is not the same as individual knowledge. They took a shortcut and relied on the study group to split up the work so each person could do less. Instead, they should have used the two-step strategy for a study group:

1. Gather and learn information independently by taking your own notes.

2. Then get together and ask one another questions to test everybody's understanding of the material. That's how your study group becomes a valuable resource.

The students who do less get less for it.

THE TAKEAWAY

- Don't cut corners when you're in a study group — you'll waste your time, big time. You'll also risk your grade.

- Use your study group to test and improve the knowledge and understanding of the material that you got on your own.

- Remember, they can help you but they can't study for you — what the group knows is not the same as what you know; you have to get that for yourself first before your group can help you.

FOLLOW-UP EXERCISE

Use the **Tips on Forming a Study Group** below to define the purpose of your group, the priorities, the expectations, the responsibilities of the members, and the logistics. You'll avoid wasting time on random chitchat — or even chaos — and you'll avoid slackers and give your team a way to score top grades.

Tips on Forming a Study Group

1. ### What is the purpose of the group?
   Make sure you know why you want to form or be in a study group. Group knowledge is not a substitute for individual knowledge. No one in your study group will take the test for you. Focus the goals of your study group so that you will help and support one another as you prepare for tests, projects, and other exercises.

2. ### What is the value of each member to the group?
   Each member is responsible for testing and understanding his or her knowledge of the material before the group discussion. Then you work as a group by splitting up the material with each member responsible for a part. That doesn't mean you just present an outline. Rather, you are the "expert of the day." It's your responsibility to lead the discussion of the material and make sure each person understands it. Make sure the other members answer questions correctly. Sometimes you will have to challenge group members with questions or contrary opinions to force discussions and justification of answers and ideas. As the "expert of the day," you must know your section of the material inside and out, and it's your responsibility to do what you can, to ensure your group understands the material as well as you do. Otherwise, you shortchange the other members.

3. ### What is not acceptable group participation?
   Spell out and agree on expectations in your very first meeting as a group. You should agree that a member is "invited" to leave if he or she does not follow through. Do not tolerate slackers or free loaders; it's unfair and their lack of contributions stirs up ill will, which can be disruptive and will make the group much less effective.

4. ***Who should be in your group?***

   Pick members who work hard to learn for themselves and who truly want to contribute. They don't have to be the smartest students in the class; in fact, it's probably better that they aren't. You need people who will be good group members, not individual performers with the smug attitude of a "star." Look for good learners *and* good teachers — people who comfortably alternate between these roles. Look before you leap! Before you ask people to join, take note of how they function in class. Do they attend every class well-prepared? Do they seem to grasp the material? Do they ask good questions? Do their answers in class make sense? Don't choose group members because you like being with them.

5. ***What are the roles of each group member?***

   Make sure everyone knows what he or she is supposed to do. In order to work effectively, groups require coordination and communication. Additionally, you will need to establish meeting places at mutually acceptable times and with an agenda in hand. Determine how you will split up the responsibilities without overloading one or two people.

6. ***How will the group work?***

   What should each group member be prepared to do at each meeting? What deliverables should be prepared for the next meeting and by whom? What will the agenda be for the next meeting?

7. ***What are the expected outcomes of the group?***

   Discuss this up front. Each member should be candid about what they expect from the group. Make sure that no one joins the group with expectations that are unrealistic or inconsistent with the group's objective.

CHAPTER 14

KNOW HOW TO BE A GOOD PLAYER AND A GOOD COACH

Teamwork divides the tasks and multiplies the success.

AUTHOR UNKNOWN

ELLIOTT WAS IN MY OFFICE, complaining about a group assignment he had to do.

"My group just doesn't want to work," he said. "There are five of us, but two of us are doing all the work. That's not fair."

"Will each member be evaluated by the other group members?" I asked him. He nodded, so I said, "That's the time to let your teacher know who is doing what and who should get credit for what."

"That's all well and good at the end of the semester, but what about now?" he said. "Who's going to do the work now? This is frustrating because I put this group together by picking people who get good grades. I figured a group of smart people means a great group."

I said, "Let your teacher know now what is happening and ask for assistance so he knows and can help — this is not the first time a group has worked this way. Your instructor is there to help you manage situations like this; don't try to do it on your own."

"You're learning some important life lessons that you can only learn by being part of a group," I said. "What does it mean to be a good player? What does it mean to be a good coach? Doing things well *yourself* as a good player requires one skill set. Supporting a group's effort or leading a group requires that you know more about accomplishing things with or through *other* people. That's a very different skill set."

I continued to refer to athletics to prove the point. I said, "There are a number of excellent professional athletes who were not good coaches. People like Bart Starr [Dallas Cowboys], Mike Singletary [Chicago Bears], Magic Johnson [Los Angeles Lakers], and Wayne Gretzky [played hockey for professional teams in Edmonton, Los Angeles, and New York] were star players but not successful coaches. Other players — some who never even played professionally — were or are excellent coaches. They include Bill Belichick [New England Patriots], Eric Spoelstra [Miami Heat], and Vince Lombardi [Chicago Bears]."

I told Elliott that his group project offered him an opportunity to learn the difference between being a coach and player. To help him learn which role suited him, we went through some basic questions:

- Can you figure out ways to get the nonperformers to do more by reassigning, rearranging, or changing their tasks?

- Do you like being the go-to guy who makes firm decisions and ensures completion of tasks?

I encouraged Elliott to see the big picture take-away. "This project is not just an assignment — it's a chance to learn about yourself as a leader. In the real world, you will start out as a player. But at some point, as you are promoted, you will be required to take on coaching and managing roles."

"As a manger, you'll need to figure out how to execute a job well through other people," I said. "Their performance will reflect how you perform as a manager. In fact, it is how your manager will evaluate you."

"So this group work is sort of an experiment," Elliott concluded.

"Yes, this is your chance to see whether you prefer a role as a coach or as a supporting team member," I answered. "This is why we require you to work in groups — to give you the opportunity to find your comfort zone. It's better for you to understand what role you play best now, instead of finding out later or even worse — never. Figuring out the valuable role you can play in a group or company is critical to your personal and professional success. Keep in mind that the best players don't always make the best coaches/teachers."

One of my students once asked me, "Was the best teacher you ever had also the smartest teacher you ever had?" I had to think a minute before I answered. "No," I responded, "I had some very smart and some very capable teachers. But sometimes the smartest people are not the most capable teachers."

It seems to reason that those who know a lot and are very smart should be better teachers, but that is not necessarily the way it works. The smartest person I went to school with was a classmate in graduate school. We were taking the same classes and frequently studied together. Reginald and I read the same material, but he always finished in half the time. To add insult to injury, he knew the material a lot better than I did. I finally asked him what his secret was.

"What secret?" he responded. He was totally unaware of how he studied, how he learned, or how he was able to use and apply what he learned. Even when I pressed him, Reginald kept saying, "I don't have a secret. I just do what has always worked for me." How can someone be so smart *but* clueless, I wondered? He really couldn't explain the how and why of his ability to learn. He just did it and aced every test.

That's why the best players—some very bright students—don't always make the best coaches or teachers; they know what to do, but they don't know how they do it, so they can't share that information with you.

We see it happen all the time in sports. The players I mentioned previously, Magic Johnson, Wayne Gretzky, are key examples. All were great players, but great coaches? Not so much. A great player or student can play well, but they can't teach others because knowledge and ability comes easily to them. They rarely have to struggle. Because of this, they don't understand why somebody else has difficulty understanding the material. A teacher may be Nobel Laureate-smart, but if they can't empathize with you when you have difficulty grasping information that comes easy to them, they are not teachers/coaches—they are only players. And because they can't relate to your situation, they may get impatient, simply because they may not know how to break down material to your level of understanding. They may try a few times to explain something and get frustrated if the class doesn't pick up on it right away. Then they send students to the library or home with instructions to work harder and concentrate more, which has the potential to transfer their frustration to you. So how do you find the best coaches? Here's a suggestion:

- When you study with people outside of class, find someone who seems better at explaining answers to the group, even if they are not the first to jump in with the answers. They are the ones you should ask to explain things to you. They know the material, and they're probably more patient.

When you find that person, you've found your coach you can count on to help you be a better student or player. And if that person is truly a great coach, they will realize that they benefit from the relationship just as much as you do, because they will be able to hone their teaching/coaching skills—a win-win.

I recently had a long and tense discussion with a student who didn't understand this. He actually brought his mother to my office to complain about his grade in the class where group work was a major portion of the grade. Students could not pass this class unless they passed the performance assessment by other team members.

First rule: don't bring your mother (or any family member) with you to discuss a grade. Not only did Mommy come to our meeting, she took the lead in the discussion. She was outraged that her son got an F. He had told her how hard he worked to support his group and how, at the end of the semester, they evaluated him based on that. I listened patiently while thinking about her son's team member evaluations that I'd reviewed in preparation for this meeting.

On the evaluation form, each student could use about one-third of a page to evaluate each team member. Mommy was in for a surprise: her son's team members had filled up the allotted comment space and then used the back of a second page to describe in detail how poorly he performed in the group. Every team member did this, not just one or two.

This was unusual, so I made a point of talking with each team member individually to ensure that Mommy's conspiracy theory wasn't true. According to his team members, her son did not participate in the group's activities; he lied to his mother about working with the team, and he had *earned* that F. When she stopped talking, I put the evaluations on my desk and then looked at her son.

"Do you want me to tell your mother the truth or will you?" I asked.

He looked down and said, "I will," then he had to tell his mother that he didn't do his work and that he had lied about it, deserved to fail the class, and would not graduate on time. His mother thought we didn't appreciate what a great coach her son was when in reality, he was really a lousy player. He let his mother, his team members, and himself down.

THE TAKEAWAY

- Look for coaches who can dig into the information with you and explain it clearly, in the way that you best understand. Your college has teachers who are on your wavelength — find them.

- Learning how to play a valuable role in a group is one of the most important skills you can learn in college and in life. Take the opportunities seriously and improve your skills as a good group player and/or coach. Your grades (and in the future, your career) may depend on your ability to play and/or coach!

- Use group work in classes to learn your role as a player and potentially a coach.

- Understand that you have to earn your right to be a member of a group that's helping you. Don't expect anything to be given to you — now or in the future.

- Ask yourself this question frequently: "How can I help the group?" not "How can the group help me?"

CHAPTER 15

GOOD PLAYERS TALK TO THE COACH

The mark of a great player is in his ability
to come back. The great champions have all
come back from defeat.

SAM SNEAD

I TOOK AN OPERATIONS RESEARCH CLASS in graduate school that was humbling for me. This class was hard, really hard—and I came to understand how hard it really was after I took my second class test. A perfect score on the test was 123. The best score in the class was only 81. My score? Reverse the digits and you have my score—that's right—18 out of 123! That 18 almost convinced me that I wouldn't see a degree. It was especially disappointing because I thought I was ready for that test. So why did the test seem as if it were written in Greek?

The class scores were so low that our teachers decided to retest us. I went to my instructor and asked about the new test. After answering a few questions, he said, "Before you came here, you should have gone over the last test as part of your preparation for the next test." I told him

I had done that and pulled out my test to discuss it. At this point, his attitude changed completely. He became laser-focused on the test and my understanding of every single part. "Do you really understand it?" he asked repeatedly. If I said yes, he would say, "Then explain it to me."

After about an hour, my professor's wife (who also worked at the school) came into the office, saying she was tired and ready to go home. Instead of cutting our session short, he surprised me by asking her to sit down so he and I could finish. Fortunately, she accommodated us both by waiting patiently while my professor and I reviewed every question for another hour.

He told me, "I don't want you to leave until I know you really understand what's on your test." By the time I left his office that evening, I did.

When I saw the second test, I understood why he hammered on every detail of the first exam — it was the same test! I could have completed it with my eyes closed. I scored a perfect 123!

My teacher didn't call me to his office after my miserable score — it was my job to make the appointment. He didn't tell me that he planned to give the same test. However, he helped me because I took the initiative and because he was a good coach. When he saw that I was determined to improve my grade, he became committed to my success. If I had not shown up to be coached, my second score would not have been much higher than the 18 I scored on the first test.

The Takeaway

- You'll never know how much your teachers can help or coach if you don't ask. You can't get help unless you go to see them — they will not chase after you; it is your responsibility to be proactive. Believe it or not, teachers love to see you take the initiative to learn and they will coach you, but they can't and won't do this for students they never see or hear from.

CHAPTER 16

KNOW YOUR GRADE
BEFORE YOU GET IT

Understanding can overcome any situation, however mysterious or insurmountable it may appear to be.

As I MENTIONED IN CHAPTER 12, you can use the syllabus for each of your classes to keep a running calculation of your current grade for the course, as well as project what your final grade might be, based on tests that you've yet to take or assignments still to be completed. This gives you a way to see how well you need to perform at any point during the course. The syllabus is a tool that many students don't always take advantage of. At the end of this chapter, I will give you a worksheet that will show you how to calculate and keep up with your grade so you know how you're really doing in a class. But first, a story . . .

In one of my classes, I had four students who were failing. I called them to my office to find out why they were doing so poorly in my class.

They all mumbled about not understanding the material, yet none of them had come to see me. I told them they could do better and I would show them how. First, however, I wanted to know if they knew what they needed to accomplish on the last two exams and on their homework assignments, in order to pass the class. My question was answered with silence. All of them were convinced that there was no way to pass the class; they had all lost hope. I asked them if they were willing to work with me if I could show them that there was a way they could still pass the class.

"Yes!" they almost shouted at the possibility of reprieve. Using the same method I'm going to share with you, I did the calculations, using information from the syllabus and their test grades to show they all needed to do B work to pass the course with a C.

"I didn't know this," one student said. "I thought there was no way to pass after bombing the first few weeks."

With a few simple calculations, they could set a realistic goal with hope of achieving it. This made the difference. Even though they weren't sure they could get B's on everything left to do during the semester, they were willing to work with me, because what I offered was a chance to pass.

I helped these students correct a few deficiencies in their study strategies and their preparation methods for tests, which are the very same strategies I'm sharing with you in this book. That was all they needed. Each student did better than B work for the rest of the semester, and they all passed the course with a C.

After the class was over, they came to see me and asked why the calculation I did wasn't on the syllabus. I told them it was and showed them how I did it.

They said, "You ought to write a book about this and put us in it!" So I did, and you're reading it!

The Takeaway

- Know where you stand in the class at all times; it can be inspiration and motivation to strive a little harder.

- Use calculations like the example below to know what you need to get the grade you want.

Follow-up Exercise

Use this link to the How Am I Doing? Worksheet to find out what you need to do to get the grade you want: **http://www.granvillesawyer. com/resources/**

By recording your test and assignment grades and multiplying them by the weighted value the professor has assigned for each test/assignment/project throughout the semester, you should be able to accurately calculate How You're Doing throughout the semester. You'll have the same tools your professor uses to calculate your grade and you will never have to guess your grade again—you will know it! An example of what can be found at the web site above is in the Appendix.

I Can Bring My Grade Point Average Up Later

Success is simple. Do what's right, the right way, at the right time.

Arnold H. Glasow

"OH YEAH—I CAN bring my grade point average up later," Wilbert said when I asked him about his 2.1 grade point average. I asked him how many hours he had taken, out of the 120 he needed for graduation.

"I have taken sixty hours so far."

"What do you want to raise your grade point average to, by the time you graduate," I asked.

Wilbert said, "I'll need at least a 3.0 GPA when I graduate, to be competitive, so that's what I'm working toward."

I said, "I agree you'll need at least a 3.0 to be competitive, but do you know what your grade point average has to be for the remaining sixty hours to get your 3.0? If your current GPA is .9 points below where you want it to be (the difference between a 3.0 - 2.1), you will have to be .9

points above your desired 3.0 for the second sixty hours you take. In other words, you will need to average a 3.90 for the last sixty hours!"

I told Wilbert, "You make your grade point average at the beginning not at the end. While averaging almost straight A's (4.0) for the rest of your courses is possible, it is not likely. Every semester counts less and less toward changing you grade point average as you accumulate hours."

"I don't understand what you mean," Wilbert said. So, I showed him a simple way to calculate and keep track of his GPA. I showed him a worksheet, where he can enter his current grade point average, the number of hours he had completed, the number of hours he needed to complete his degree requirements, and the grade point average he wanted to graduate with. The worksheet showed Wilbert the required grade point average for the hours he had left, confirming that stretch figure of 3.90 I had given him already.

Wilbert said, "I have my work cut out for me. I just wish I had known this earlier."

You have an advantage over Wilbert, because you are reading this before or early in your college career. You'll find the College In Four Years Grade Point Average Estimator I shared with Wilbert by following the link below—just plug in your grades as you get them and you will always know where you are and what it will take to get you where you want to go: **http://granvillesawyer.com/resources/**. An example of this worksheet is in the Appendix.

THE TAKEAWAY

- Start working toward the grade point average you need to graduate with, on the first day of class your freshman year. Front load your GPA with good grades earned early in your college career.

PART IV

Knowing How to Learn

CHAPTER 18

SEE IT FOUR TIMES TO LEARN IT

A baseball swing is a very finely tuned
instrument. It is repetition, and more repetition, then a little more after that.

REGGIE JACKSON

ILLIAM, one of my more inquisitive students, once asked
me whether the material covered in class that day would
ever show up in another class.

"You will see this material about four times before you graduate,"
I said.

"Let me get this straight," William said. "If you're going to show me
the same thing four times during the four years it takes to get my degree,
then why don't you show it to me once and let me graduate in one year?"

"Because you don't understand why you're in college."

"Of course I do — to get a degree."

I told William to have a seat — he was about to get an education.

"A degree is just a means to an end," I said, "not the end objective
itself. The degree is confirmation that you did well enough to graduate,

but there's a more important objective to accomplish. People who have jobs to fill are looking for candidates who can answer questions and solve problems. In other words, they want to know what you can do, *not* just what you know. What you can do depends on how well you can apply what you know in different situations, at different times. To be able to apply knowledge, you need to see it applied more than once, so you need more than one semester to collect all the knowledge you'll need. Then you have to demonstrate how it can be used in multiple situations, so you have to practice, time and time again. You have to work on problems that have already been solved and others that have never been solved."

"I'm still not seeing it," my student said. I pulled out the sequence sheet of business courses required for his degree and laid it out in steps:

- The first is Introduction to Business. Touching on all facets of business, it broadly describes each discipline within the subject. This overview helps students zero in on a major.

- The next courses give an overview of each major in the business school. All business students must take these courses.

- The first course in each major follows those courses. An example would be Accounting 101, taken by everyone; Intermediate Accounting 201 is only taken by accounting majors.

- Then, the next set of classes make up the remaining business major courses. (See the **Map Your Courses: Sample Class Sequence Diagram** on page 43 for an example of how these courses can fit together.)

"As you see," I said, "one class builds on another. With each class, you learn more about how to apply knowledge introduced in the first course, to answer questions and solve problems. That's your four times — if you can figure out how to learn this sequence in a year, you're outta here. Or you can take it all in, understand, apply and expand on it, and graduate with valuable knowledge and skills that you can successfully apply for the rest of your life."

"Four times," William said, "got it."

THE TAKEAWAY

- Whatever your major may be, recognize each time that you see or encounter material and solve certain problems. Understand how you are supposed to master the classes and the material to reach each level. The fifth time may be your first job or first semester in grad school. Be ready!

CHAPTER 19

How to Know When Your Answer Just Doesn't Look Right

Understanding concepts enables you to see more and do more and communicate more of what you already know.

Dr. Granville M. Sawyer Sr.

A SCIENCE INSTRUCTOR ONCE ASKED HER class if they had ever done a problem and thought, "The answer doesn't look right." Most of the students said yes. Then she asked, "How did you know?"

No one could offer a clear explanation.

"We just knew," they said. These students understood deeper problem solving at the conceptual level, not just the mechanical. Unfortunately, some students do not reach this more sophisticated level of understanding.

The familiar question, "Will this be on the test?" means students are working at the mechanical level and will try memorizing just enough material to pass the test; I talked about the mechanic's approach a little in the Takeaway for Chapter 11. When you study like a mechanic for a test, you usually forget everything you learned by the next day, because you don't fully understand the material and can't apply what you learned. You never understood the information on a conceptual level.

If you know and understand the concepts, you have a feel for the "rightness" of a problem's answer. You may not know for sure what the answer is, but you do know when you're close and when you aren't. You know when an answer just doesn't look right; you can figure it out.

It doesn't matter whether you're in a science class or an economics class or whether you're at home trying to figure out how much carpet you need for your living room. If you grasp the main idea of what you are doing, you're more likely to come up with the right answer.

Two of my students needed a minimum score on the final in order to pass one of my classes with a C. A lower mark required repeating the class. They were sure about one problem-solution. I could tell by how they wrote the answer. Everything was super neat — no erasures and clearly circled answers. In other words, they nailed this one, or so they thought.

In fact, they both made mistakes that clearly showed they didn't understand the concept behind the problem. The approach they took was fundamentally wrong; it applied to a different type of problem. A student who understood the concept would have at least known that the answer "didn't look right." When I showed them their test results, they were amazed. Neither had a clue about how they should have solved the problems, and I'm sorry to say that both students failed the test and had to repeat the course. One even appealed his grade as unfair, but administration threw that appeal out — they knew it "didn't look right."

THE TAKEAWAY

- Remember that you came to college for an education, not just grades. Get an understanding of concepts and principles so you can answer real-world questions and solve real-world problems. That is the foundation you'll need for a real education, and it is what employers want to see—critical thinking. Don't be surprised when you start to interview for a job and you get questions that require you to evaluate a problem, come up with assumptions, and produce a solution on the spot.

- Critical thinking will also help you develop a successful business of your own, should you choose to become an entrepreneur. If you provide clear answers and solutions to clients' questions and problems, you'll beat the competition.

- Think big! Get the overarching concept. Then, as you work through the small stuff, you'll find your way, feel the rightness, and boom! You'll know the answer.

CHAPTER 20

ASK THE SMARTEST QUESTION YOU CAN: "HOW DID I KNOW?"

The wise man doesn't give the right answers,
he poses the right questions.

CLAUDE LEVI-STRAUSS

I WAS EATING LUNCH ONE DAY when an angry student burst into the break room to talk with my friend, Dr. Richards, who is her advisor. Corinne had taken her first accounting test and flunked it. Dr. Richards had just taken a bite of her sandwich, which gave over-charged Corinne time to blow through her scenario.

"My grade was not even close to passing, and I don't think most of the class passed either. It's the teacher! He just can't make the stuff we go over in class understandable. I studied the material at home, I did the homework problems, *and* I asked questions in class. But when I read the problems on the test, I was sure the teacher had made a mistake and thought that this must be a test for another class. I didn't know how to do any of the problems because they didn't look anything like what we had been studying." Dr. Richards didn't have much time, because her next class started in five minutes. She talked with Corinne briefly about working harder in class and asking the teacher for assistance; that was all she could do for the moment, she had to excuse herself and head to class.

Corinne was still wound up, so I asked her to sit down and relax a minute. Then I asked whether her instructor answered questions in class, especially about the homework problems.

"Yes, he does," Corinne said. "If we ask him to go over a problem in class, he will do it."

I said, "Tell me how that works."

"It's pretty simple," Corinne replied, slowing down her words. "Someone asks about a problem, and the teacher puts the solution on the board and asks whether we understand it."

"Do you?"

"Usually I do," Corinne said. "If I don't, I tell him that I don't understand the solution on the board, and he answers my questions." Then she tensed up again. "That's what was really frustrating about the test."

"What do you mean?" I asked.

"One of the problems came from the homework. I couldn't even do that one!"

"What happened? I thought you understood how to work them."

"I thought I did," Corinne said.

"What did your instructor say about your test scores?"

"He was angry," she said. "He didn't understand why—after going through most of the homework problems in class and answering all the questions we had—the scores were so low. He asked us why, and all we could say was that we didn't know."

"So your teacher is mad because he thinks you aren't trying, and you're mad because you think he's not teaching," I said. "The end result is a failing grade on your test."

"Have you been to my class?"

"Not a foot in the door," I said.

"So what are you, some kind of psychic?!" She looked amazed. "That's the only way you could know so much about my class, the teacher, and us."

"No, I'm not a psychic, but I've been a college professor long enough to know a few things," I said. "Let's break this down again. You ask your teacher about a problem."

"Yes," she said, "then he goes to the board and works the problem."

"OK, does that really answer your question?" I asked, digging a little deeper. "In other words, does seeing the solution help you know how to recognize a similar problem when you see it again?"

"I don't know what you mean," she said.

"Think about what you told me about the test—that you didn't know how to start the problems."

At that point, Corinne caught on to what I was saying. "We never discussed this in class or out of class when we are studying together," she said. "We just wanted to get to the answer."

"In your next class, approach your professor this way: 'I don't know how to get started with this problem,'" I said. "Ask your teacher what *type* of problem it is. Ask him how you should be able to recognize it, when you see a similar one on the next test. Let him help you see this and, in the process, understand better how to state problems in ways that are more likely to help you recognize them."

"This is great," said Corinne. "I'm going to start doing this for every problem."

About three weeks later, I bumped into Corrine in the hallway. She was in a much better mood. "I tried what you suggested," she said, "and it worked just as you said it would. When the teacher went over a problem in class, I asked, 'How did you know how to get started?'"

"I bet he was glad you asked."

"Definitely!" said Corinne. "We went carefully through the problem, and then he showed us what to look for in any problem like it."

"So you got your communication on track," I said.

"Did you have another test?" I asked.

She broke out in a big smile and said, "As a matter of fact I did and I made a 97 on it—just by doing what you suggested."

About two weeks after the semester ended, Corinne called me to say that she got a B in that accounting class. It was a great accomplishment to go from an F, to passing with a much higher grade. I didn't tell her this, but the course she was taking has a first-time failure rate of sixty percent!

Later that week, I had lunch with Dr. Anderson, a math professor who teaches the first-level general-education math course that all students must pass. He told me about a question posed by one of his freshmen students, Andrea. She asked him what problems were going to be on the upcoming test. He gave her advice similar to what I told Corinne.

"I can't tell you exactly what the problems will be, but I will give you a chance to choose the types of problems yourself," Dr. Anderson said. Andrea couldn't believe her luck. She thought Dr. Anderson would allow her to make up her own test!

"Well, not quite," he said. "Look at this group of problems and pick out the ones you're familiar with from the homework. See which ones you can solve. I'll make up the test based on the problems you choose." Andrea carefully looked over the problems he put before her and said, "This is a trick, isn't it?"

"No, it is not a trick," said Dr. Anderson. "These problems came from the chapters we covered; they just weren't assigned to you for homework."

"That's not possible," Andrea said. "I don't recognize any of them. We didn't go over problems like this and you didn't assign any like this!"

"I did," said Dr. Anderson. He went through several problems, showing Andrea exactly how they related to the homework problems she had done and how to work them, using the information she already knew.

"I don't understand," said Andrea. "When you do the problems, everything makes sense and they are easy to understand. But I have trouble doing this on my own." She was clearly flustered.

Dr. Anderson methodically guided her, "Tell me how you study these problems at home."

"I read a problem and go through the chapter to see if there are any examples like it," she said. "Then I find the formula I need to do the problem. After that, I figure out how to use the formula to get the answer. When I can, I check my answer by looking at the answers in the back of the book."

"Then what? Is that all you do with that problem?" He asked.

"I just make sure the answer is right and then go on to the next problem and work it the same way," she replied.

"So why didn't you recognize the problems I just showed you?" he asked. "They're like the ones you've done before."

"Dr. Anderson, I just don't know," she said. "It's obvious I'm missing something here."

"The missing piece is a simple question: *How did you know?*'" Andrea still looked confused. Dr. Anderson spelled it out in four steps. Once she finished a problem, she needed to ask:

- How did I know what kind of problem this is when I started to solve it?

- How did I know how to start this problem?

- What element(s) do I recognize that always help me know what type of problem this is?

- What is the strategy I can use to solve any problem like this?

"No one ever told me about these questions," said Andrea. "I never thought about problems that way. I thought I was done when I got the right answer."

"You're never finished with a problem just because you got the right answer," said Dr. Anderson, reinforcing his point. "If you work 1,000 problems for homework, by relying on guesswork, then you won't understand problem 1,001 when it pops up on a test. You must ask and answer the four questions I gave you to be sure you truly understand the problem and recognize the type of problem it is. Try it yourself. If you need help at first, come see me, and I can show you how."

THE TAKEAWAY

- Always ask and answer the four questions to understand the how and why of each problem. And you can't cut corners — you have to read the chapter before trying to solve problems. The content in the chapter breaks down every type of problem you'll encounter in homework and on tests. If you understand what the author of the textbook wrote about a problem, it's going to be a lot easier to recognize a similar problem when you see it again, and chances are, you will see it again on a test.

- If you can't follow through on your own, your teacher is your best resource — he or she can guide you through Dr. Anderson's steps. This is how students get good grades in quantitative subjects, because they can recognize a problem when they see it again. That's the hard part, but once you've mastered that, you can go through the "plug and chug" method. You plug in the number and chug out the answer. Easy . . . or at least, easier!

CHAPTER 21

THIS IS WHY YOU HATE WORD PROBLEMS

A good decision is based on knowledge and not on numbers.

PLATO

URING A CONVERSATION WITH MY student, Ted, he told me how he hated word problems.

"On our tests, why can't you just give us the problems ready to work without having to deal with all of the words?" I answered him with a word problem.

"How would you like it if instead of food coming to you the normal way, it all came to you as a predigested paste, that you just squeezed into your mouth and swallowed?"

"Doc, it's close to lunch time and you're ruining my appetite," Ted said. "I would never want to eat anything that way, and besides, what does that have to do with word problems?"

"In the work world, you start with someone's description of a problem to be solved or a question to be answered. We don't talk in numbers,

Ted," I said. "Have you ever been greeted by a friend who said '63, 88, 99, 53' instead of 'How are you doing?'"

"No," said Ted.

"Of course not! You can't sit around and wait for someone to 'predigest' the words and create a problem 'ready to work' and then give it to you. No one in life, school, or work is going to do that. It's the words in the problem that help you recognize a type of problem when you see it in the real world."

"I'm not quite connecting the dots," said Ted.

"Being able to recognize a problem when you see it again makes life easier to negotiate, helps you make better grades in school and will make you valuable to potential employers," I said. "If you're a 'mechanic,' instead of a critical thinker, you will always need someone else—your parents, your professors, a supervisor—to tell you what to do. Especially in these times, employers can't afford to hire mechanics. They want you primed, trained, ready to hit the ground running, ready to make a contribution to their bottom line. Do you want to be a mechanic or someone who manages mechanics, who is the decision maker and makes more money?" I asked.

"Doc, that's a no brainer! I don't want to spend my professional career being a mechanic."

"I knew you'd be able to figure out the answer to that word problem."

The Takeaway

- Here's the key to coming up with answers and solutions, especially quantitative ones: read, understand the words, and then crunch the numbers. Don't try to do it the other way. It's much harder.

- Use your understanding to answer the question, "How did I know?"

CHAPTER 22

YOU NEED YOUR OWN OUTLINE

Actually, all education is self-education. A
teacher is only a guide, to point out the way,
and no school, no matter how excellent, can
give you education. What you receive is like
the outlines in a child's coloring book. You
must fill in the colors yourself.

LOUIS L'AMOUR

(AMERICAN WRITER, BEST-SELLING AUTHOR, 1908–1988)

I N CHAPTER 11, I WROTE about using your textbook to create an
outline you can study. Let's revisit that concept but this time with
a little more detail. Though you may not be in graduate school, this
story about Sheila, an MBA student, will help you understand how to
create your own outlines — information that you can use now and later.

Sheila was preparing to take her comprehensive exam for the third
time; she had failed it on her first two attempts. If she failed it a third
time, she would not get her degree, so this was definitely crunch time.

I told Sheila, "You have to create your own outline to study. You can't use one somebody else created for you."

"I know. I did that for the last test," she said, her voice a little shaky. "I got outlines from friends who had passed the test, and I thought I could just use those to get ready for the test last time. It didn't work."

"To do this right, you have to prepare your *own* study guide, one that perfectly fits your learning style. No one else can do this for you, because they don't know how you learn." I asked Sheila if she had ever taken a test where the teacher let her bring in whatever she wanted on a three-by-five note card.

"Yes, a couple of times."

I asked her what preparing that note card was like.

"At first, I wrote smaller than I thought possible, to cram the information on my first card," she said. "There was so much, I could barely read it, so I had to cut it back. I looked at what we needed to know, studying it carefully to see if it should be on my card. I must have redone that card six or seven times and read over the assigned chapters at least that many times."

"That's exactly what I thought you did," I said. "Now tell me how much of what was on the card you used during the test."

"Come to think of it, not that much." I asked her why she didn't use the card more, since she took so long to get it just right.

"I didn't need to," she answered. "I knew what was on it already. There were just a few things I needed to look at –" she thought a minute "– I learned the material by writing the card."

"That's exactly right, and your teacher knew it," I said. "He knew how hard you would work preparing your 'cheat sheet' and how much you would learn in the process. That's why you have to do your own outline for the test."

Sheila said, "I've done outlines before, so I know how to do this."

"I'm sure you have, but I want you to take a different approach this time," I said. "First, I want you to remember that the objective for your outline is to translate sentences in your book to words in your outline that represent sentences or concepts from your book."

"Like a code?"

"Sort of," I said. "The idea is not to write down everything you want to know. You want to write only the key words that you have to remember to write the sentences, in your own words, that answer questions on the test. Don't try to remember or mimic exactly what the author wrote."

"Not to worry," Sheila said, "that guy is too long-winded."

"You're doing an outline, not a script for a play where every word is there," I said. "Think of the words in your outline as spark plugs. They ignite automatic recollection of thoughts that you convert to sentences."

"OK, less writing," she said. "Sounds good to me."

"That means, of course, you must remember everything in your out-line—absolutely everything you write, verbatim. You've got to know your outline so well that you can see it with your eyes closed."

"I guess I need to choose my words carefully."

"Yes, that's it! Just as you had to be careful about how much infor-mation fit on the index card," I said. "If you forget a word, you'll forget a sentence or a thought, not just a word."

"That would be a nightmare," she said, her voice quavering. I knew she was thinking about failing her last test.

"Just remember this," I reassured her. "You're doing just what you did with that index card. For that card, you converted sentences and concepts in your book to just the minimum words and numbers you needed, to use the information on the test. When you did it, two things happened: you learned the material and remembered what you learned when you took the test. That's exactly what you need to do to pass your comp exam."

Sheila used all the information I gave her on drafting an outline for the comprehensive examination. It was her last shot. She went home and spent a week going over all the textbook chapters, her class notes, her study notes, and the list of items to study for the test. She worked hard summarizing this mountain of information and brought me the results.

"I really tried to summarize, but I think the outline is a bit too long to memorize." She was right—it was thirty-seven pages!

"This is good for a first pass," I said. "Now look at what you have and try again. Don't go back to the book or your notes. You're finished with them, so make sure everything you think is important is in your outline. We'll focus on the outline only."

"But isn't that a little bit risky?" Sheila asked. "Suppose I missed something?"

"That's a chance you have to take," I said. "You can't know everything and we don't expect you to. That's why when we give you the guide that details what the exam will cover, it doesn't include every topic. You should have used that information to guide you."

Sheila hesitated. "Maybe I should just go back through everything one more time."

"You can do that as many times as you want," I said, "however, at some point, you'll have to close the books and put away the notes. You'll have to rely only on your outline. That's as much as you can remember."

"OK. I think everything is in there. What's next?"

"Look at your outline again, just as you did your index card," I said. "Make sure there are only words that cue recollection of sentences or concepts. Think of the words as sentences, so if you want to write a five-sentence answer to a question, decide what five words should be in your outline. Don't exceed that number unless you absolutely have to for complete recollection."

The next outline was fifteen pages, instead of thirty-seven. "Now that's progress," I praised.

"It wasn't as hard as I thought it would be, once I started thinking about words representing sentences or thoughts."

"Now try again," I said, "but this time, eliminate any words you don't need to remember, in order to write complete thoughts."

"How am I going to know that?"

"This is the time for you to start writing," I explained. "You practice writing answers based just on what is in your outline, nothing else. Practice, practice, practice! You will see what needs to be in the outline and what doesn't."

"That's going to take a long time."

"You have to put in the time now to pass the test later," I said. "You can't do what you did before and expect a different result."

The next outline was ten pages — every word chosen carefully and every page packed with valuable information. Her outline was ready. The way she talked about the material showed that she had truly learned it in the process. Now she was ready for the final step.

"You have done an outstanding job," I said. "You have only one more thing to do. You must memorize this outline completely so you can quickly recall the information in an organized way. Focus only on this so you will be ready for the test." She was ready. She passed her comp exam and earned her MBA.

Follow-up Exercise

I gave Sheila three short passages and outlines as examples she could follow. Go to **http://www.granvillesawyer.com/resources/** to see sample outlines of **both quantitative and non-quantitative material.** The information on the web site is also in the Appendix.

The Takeaway

- You have to put your own spin on an outline, to make it work just for you.

- Creating an outline for yourself takes time and effort, so be prepared to work for your success.

- Writing an outline is not limited to test preparation; it is applicable to what you plan to do in the future. A well-done outline distills a lot of information into a short comprehensive document that you can use as a quick reference, instead of dragging out a lot of original material to sift through. When your professor, boss, or anyone else needs a fast answer, you'll be able to respond—pronto.

CHAPTER 23

PowerPoint Me in the Right Direction

There are always three speeches, for every one you actually gave. The one you practiced, the one you gave, and the one you wish you gave.

Dale Carnegie

"Yes," I said, "every student will have to present their project to the class at the end of the semester."

Tom looked visibly worried by this. After class he said, "Doctor Sawyer, is there *anything* else I can do to substitute for the presentation? I'm just no good at standing in front of a group speaking—I get nervous and confused. I can't seem to remember what I wanted to say or how I wanted to say it."

"What if you had notes or even a set of PowerPoint slides—would that help?" I asked.

Tom was ecstatic. "That would be great. PowerPoint slides will definitely make a difference. Thanks, Doctor Sawyer!"

During our next class meeting, I let everyone know that they could use PowerPoint for their presentations, and I got the same response that Tom gave me from everyone else in the class. They all said that being able to use PowerPoint would make the difference.

"Why do you think this will help so much?" I asked.

"We can put what we want to say on the PowerPoint slides and read them in class," they said.

I said, "No you can't. Reading what is right in front of someone is one of the most irritating things you can do in a presentation. Everyone in the audience can read; they don't need you to read for them. If that's what you're planning to do, you could just hand them your presentation and sit down!"

"So what are we supposed to do?" the class said in unison.

I said, "Outline your project with no more than three to five bulleted discussion points on one slide. Use the bullets as talking points, not as a script to be read." To be sure they understood, I requested that they submit drafts of the PowerPoint slides before the presentations; a significant portion of their grades was riding on this presentation, so it had to be right. When I reviewed the presentations, the students hit the important points in their projects, along with all of the other points. It was clear that they did not know how to summarize accurately and comprehensively, nor did they know how to present their summaries in a conversational way that suggested they knew what they were talking about.

I suggested that they use the outlining techniques for test material that they had been using the whole semester. (Examples of this outlining technique can be found on **http://granvillesawyer.com/resources/**.)

Their response? "Why would we do that? This presentation isn't a test?"

"But the outlines you did are exactly what you need for your PowerPoint slides—they are bullets that summarize what you wanted to know. They were not everything you wanted to know, but they were enough to jog your memory so you could write *or talk* about the material in a knowledgeable way."

The students who had used the outlining techniques effectively immediately understood what I was talking about. They applied their outlining skills to produce excellent PowerPoint slides, which they could easily talk from to effectively present their projects.

The Takeaway

- Outlining techniques are a perfect way to prepare for a presentation. You'll know the material backwards and forwards, so you can concentrate on your delivery and audience.

- Your class/audience will not suffer through 50 of the most boring minutes of their lives while you read every slide to them, one tiresome word at a time. The PowerPoint rule is three to five bullet points per slide! A short outline with few words packs the punch you are looking for when delivering an effective presentation.

CHAPTER 24

Use the Gut Check: It Will Always Tell You the Truth

You have to master not only the art of listening to your head, you must also master listening to your heart and listening to your gut.

Carly Fiorina

"How do you know when you're ready to take a test?" asked Gwen, a worried student. "I don't mind working hard and putting in the time to get ready, but I've never known a way to figure out when I'm really ready. Sometimes I spend too much time studying and, unfortunately, sometimes I haven't spent enough time."

"You're not the first student—undergraduate straight through to graduate—to feel that way. My friend Olivia once faced this question, when we were both preparing for an exam in our doctoral programs. She was a semester ahead of me and always studied alone, because she didn't know the other students who were taking the exam. She read and analyzed all the material and scoured all the published papers that she thought would help her, and after all that, she thought she was ready. But she failed because she didn't do the Gut Check."

"The *what?*"

"The Gut Check—it's like a checkup," I said, "Only you're the doctor. Olivia needed a way to check her readiness for the test. She talked to a professor, who told her about the Gut Check and it helped her survive that second test." Here's how it works:

- Once you think you have prepared well for a test, find a quiet place where you can sit comfortably and close your eyes.

- See yourself in the moment of the test with the exam in front of you.

- See your hand come down and write your name on the test.

- Don't think—just feel.

- Does your heart start to race?

- Do your palms get sweaty?

- Does your butt pucker up a little?

"All of these responses are triggered by the same emotion—fear," I said. "Whether you want to know it or not, your heart and your gut are telling you the truth: you're not ready. You can't think your way around fear."

"Olivia filled me in on the Gut Test when it was time for me to take my comprehensive exams," I said. "She put it this way, 'When you're at home, relaxed and comfortable, it's easy to convince yourself that you're ready. But if you're not, you'll get to the test, and fear will kick in. Thirty percent of what you think you know will disappear.'"

"How do you know when to use the Gut Check?" asked Gwen.

"You can use it along the way, to test your readiness multiple times, and you can use it at the end, as a final check. Whenever you do the

Gut Check, you have to allow yourself some time for more studying if you need it. Like Olivia, I used it multiple times, including a final check two weeks before my test. How much time you allow will depend on how much material your test will cover. The Gut Check didn't fail me; it helped me realize when I was ready, and I took my exam and passed. To this day, I never do anything that important without checking the gut first!

The Takeaway

- Incorporate the Gut Check into your pre-test routine. It works now for tests, and it will work later when you're prepping for job interviews, critical meetings, and client presentations.

- The Gut Check is in addition to, and not a substitute for, talking with your professors, mentors, and managers who can guide you when preparing for tests and other performance assessments in your academic and professional life.

- Know that the Gut Check is not a substitute for good time management. You have to work hard and work smart in college. Here's some good advice on time management: http://www.cob.sjsu.edu/ nellen_a/time_management.htm.

PART V

THERE'S MORE TO COLLEGE THAN A DEGREE

CHAPTER 25

YOU HAVE TIME TO BE HAPPY

The best thing about the future is that it comes one day at a time.

ABRAHAM LINCOLN

ARTHUR, A STUDENT WHO WAS graduating in history, came to see me to discuss his future. We had met a couple of years before, when he was hanging out with some of his friends majoring in business.

"I'm glad to be graduating, but not necessarily in liberal arts," he said. "I like my major all right, but it's not my true passion."

"Why not?"

"History came easily to me, so I thought it was the way to go. I've been preparing to teach grades nine through twelve, but when I did my student teaching, I started to have doubts."

"Will you be able to make a career in a liberal arts profession if you have no passion for it? Can you do that year after year?" I asked.

"I don't know," said Arthur. "That's why I'm here. I still like history, but teaching didn't fit me as well as I thought it would." I asked him if he had any other options.

"My cousin is finally breaking in as a musician. We grew up together, so we're very close. When I first started college, Frank's band was mostly local. But now they're playing all over the region. He asked me to work for him. That really excited me."

I needed Arthur to give that opportunity a more holistic assessment. "What responsibilities would you have working for your cousin? Are you a musician too?"

"No, no," he said, "I would manage things, like making sure that everyone who is supposed to have tickets got them. I'd handle parking, the munchies, and water. Oh yeah, and I make sure there's enough lead time to set up — like the system sound check."

"Anything else?" I wanted to make sure that Arthur had thought this through.

"The contracts. I would have to go over the details, like the place, date, and time. The description of the show and how long it would last. Payment and cancellation. Stuff like that."

"I don't know much about the music business," I probed, "but there's probably more to it than that. Things like health and safety, following state laws, riders. Are you sure you know enough?"

"I'm lucky," Arthur said, "the current manager is hanging around long enough to show me the ropes. And, I took a couple of basic business courses, because I once thought about majoring in business."

I didn't say anything for a few moments; I wanted him to think some more.

"I want to do this for now," he said. "The contracts are pretty straight-forward at this point."

"Do you have any kind of real-life business experience?" I asked.

"Before I came to school, I took a year off. I was sort of burned out, so I opted out one year to work at CarMax. I picked up some basics."

"Like what?"

Arthur rattled off a few skills: "Reviewing vehicle purchases, apprais-ing trade-ins, keeping up with title documents. Maintaining all DMV and title documents for about 250 vehicles. Handling accounts payable and bank deposits. My uncle managed the place, so he taught me a lot."

"You're obviously a disciplined person, because you've done well in college," I said. "You're on the right track. But could you really make a living working for your cousin?"

"Not a lot of money at first," Arthur said. "But I think it would be something I really want to try."

Now we were getting somewhere. "How old are you?" I asked.

"Twenty-three."

"Do you know you're rich?"

"I sure don't feel that way. I barely make ends meet every month. You know, the ramen noodle diet the last five days of the month."

"I don't mean financially rich," I said. "You're rich in something more precious than money — time. Most of your life is ahead of you."

"I guess so."

"Really think about it. You have time to be happy. You can't make time; only God can do that. It's more important than money because money can't buy it."

"You sound like my dad," Arthur laughed.

"He's been around long enough to understand this. There is another important difference between time and money. A friend of mind once said, 'Yesterday is a cancelled check, tomorrow is a promissory note. The only cash you have is today. Use it wisely.'"

"That makes sense to me. Maybe this job for my cousin is OK for now," Arthur said.

"Well, it is experience," I commented.

"Yes, but it may not provide me with a living in the long run." Now Arthur was thinking more.

"You have time, but you're going to have to do more in your professional career to become better qualified."

"Maybe I'll go back to doing something in business, especially if I do this work for my cousin for a while. Maybe I'll find out," Arthur said.

"I think you will. At this point in your life, you can always go back to school. You could get an MBA or even a PhD. You have the intellect, skills, and time to do either—or both! And I can help you look into scholarships, so you could get your degree on someone else's dime."

"If I go that way," said Arthur, "I want to do more than plain business. Something more creative than being closed in by four walls in a corporate office."

"OK, let's push the creative."

"What do you mean?"

"Let's say you work for your cousin for a while to get some practical experience. Then you could go to law school and work on a combination of a law degree and an MBA; there are several programs like this. They would give you expertise in areas you would need, in order to manage artists and entertainers."

Arthur was surprised. "I didn't know about programs like that."

"It's a big commitment, but, remember, you have the wealth of time." Arthur is the kind of person who can think for himself. He just needed some ideas and a little push.

"I'm going to find out more about that so we can talk again," he said with growing excitement.

I knew he would follow through. "I'm looking forward to it," I said.

Though Arthur was looking at a path that combined his interest in the entertainment field and the graduate degrees he would need, I knew he would still appreciate his liberal arts background. Without the pressure of teaching and his lack of passion for it, he could still read and enjoy history and find creative ways to apply it to whatever he chose in life.

Not long after I had this conversation with Arthur, I traveled to Ethiopia with a group of students, including Arthur. The purpose of the trip was to expose students to the business and cultural environment in a developing African country. Our general goal was to stimulate the students' curiosity about the world outside of their own environment and give them an experience that would broaden their perspective throughout their lives. With Arthur's background in history, his interest in music, and the trip's emphasis on business, he returned from the Ethiopian experience with a more creative outlook on how he could combine his degree, his desire to work with his cousin, and a business discipline. The trip helped him to realize that by taking time and initiative, he could find a way to let his passion drive him to experiences that equal a happy life.

THE TAKEAWAY

- Be brave enough to be happy. Pursue the experiences and goals that really interest you, but think them through. Let your passion drive you, but always have a plan.

- Think about how you can make college an adventure, not just courses to take and complete. School-related travel in and outside the country is an excellent way to do this.

CHAPTER 26

Be Liberal But Be Smart

Be prepared and be honest.

John Wooden

THOUGH THE CURRENT STATE OF the economy might make you think otherwise, students majoring in the liberal arts can still follow their passion. However, the economy today demands that liberal arts graduates think in very practical terms. Advisors often tell these students to get a small dose of other skills that can lead to careers in marketing, sales, business, social media, nonprofit development, and more. For example, English majors may have a passion for literature, but more are picking up courses in technical writing, graphic design, and basic business — especially when they are not headed to graduate school. A business-related internship also helps liberal arts majors stretch their skills.

Recent articles in business publications even underscore that the liberal arts can be a pathway to rewarding careers — both personally and financially. The Association of American Medical Colleges (AAMC) reported that medical schools accepted fifty-one percent of humanities majors and forty-five percent of social sciences majors who applied in

2010, saying, "Admission committee members know that medical students can develop the essential skills of acquiring, synthesizing, applying, and communicating information through a wide variety of academic disciplines." [6]

In fact, an acquaintance of mine who interviews med school candidates told me he isn't looking for science robots. "I ask about the latest books they've read, their favorite electives, and where they've volunteered and why. Even with advanced technology, we need doctors who can zero in on a patient's problems with a human touch — that requires good communication and interest beyond narrow knowledge."

Forbes magazine even commented on the types of students being admitted to law school, saying they represented a wide range of majors, even philosophy and anthropology. Like medical schools, law schools also value liberal arts skills.[7]

In Chapter 2, I mentioned a business recruiter who said he looked for candidates who could communicate and came dressed to play, and then they could learn the rest. I know plenty of hiring managers who value people who can think, write, analyze, and speak persuasively. The current trend is moving away from corporate training and development; companies may be willing to teach a new employee the skill to do the company's work the way the company wants it done, but they will not spend the time or money to teach basic work or life skills. Acquiring those skills is your job in college and after college; it is your responsibility to learn the basics on your own.

All of this goes back to what I stressed earlier: a true college education is not simply collecting a bunch of credits; it is understanding the "jumble in life" and that there is no singular science part or math part or language part. If you're truly serious about your college career, you'll

---

6 http://www.usnews.com/education/blogs/medical-school-admissions-doctor/2013/09/11/
choose-the-right-undergraduate-major-for-medical-school, Choose the Right
Undergraduate Major for Medical School, U.S. News and World Report
7 "Does Your Major Matter?", Skorton, David and Altschuler, Glen, www.forbes.com/
sites/collegeprose/2012/10/29/does-your-major-matter

learn the critical thinking that goes with all these areas. You won't be cramming facts into your head the night before a test just to pass and only to forget it all the next day.

Another student, Mary, is living proof of someone who can major in the liberal arts while coming up with a smart plan. Her passion is theatre and she is determined to head to New York and chase her dreams. She is willing to room with two other people in an apartment probably no larger than 500 square feet, audition tirelessly, and take more acting lessons—all while waiting tables at an upscale restaurant.

After a talk with her advisor at the end of her sophomore year, she came up with a backup plan: a minor in communications. If acting did not come through as quickly as she wanted, she could rely on the right concentration of courses that might land her a position as a copywriter, communications specialist, journalist, ad agency account executive, publicist, or even a local TV reporter.

Mary's advisor also showed her how to sell professional skills acquired in college. Theatre majors are problem solvers and they're versatile. The must know how to build scenery, hang lights, and make props—sometimes in limited space and with low budgets. They do not view a task as something to "get over with"; instead they have trained in a world that demands creativity, collaboration, innovation, and fortitude. Think about it. Actors must follow the director's rules, cooperate closely in a group (fellow actors and crew), be flexible with script changes, learn lines quickly, and meet a deadline—that opening curtain every night. They might be actors in one play and work with the crew for another. They spend many weeknights rehearsing for plays, so they must study efficiently. Think about how closely these skills align with so many other types of work, from inside a corporation to on your own as an entrepreneur. With a communications minor, Mary has additional skills that can apply to a variety of industries. Even if she does not make it on the Great White Way, she can fulfill her passion in so many different ways.

The Takeaway

- Pursue your passion in life, but understand the importance of having a backup plan—just in case there are times when passion doesn't pay the rent.

CHAPTER 27

KNOW WHY WANTING CAN BE BETTER THAN HAVING

Success is getting and achieving what you want. Happiness is wanting and being content with what you get.

BERNARD MELTZER

A STUDENT CAME TO MY OFFICE a few semesters ago for help with a homework assignment. She noticed a poster of Porsche automobiles I had on my wall and commented, "I want one of those too." So I asked her which one was her favorite. She said, "The red convertible. It's perfect for me."

I said, "Do you ever dream about having the car and driving it?"

She said, "Of course! Those are very pleasant thoughts!" I asked her to describe what a perfect day with her Porsche would be like. "Really, seriously?" she asked.

"Yes, tell me what that ideal day would be like."

"I'm driving with the top down with my favorite music playing," she said.

"Is the weather perfect? Is your favorite person next to you? Is the tank full of gas?"

"Yes, yes, and yes!"

"Now hold that vision," I said, "and let me ask you a few more questions. Are you worried about paying for the car, as well as maintaining and insuring it?" My student's smile diminished a bit. "Are you concerned about damaging it in an accident or the car being vandalized?"

"Of course not," she answered, "what kind of day dream would include stuff like that?"

That day was cold and blustery with a mix of rain and snow falling, making the roads treacherous and snarling traffic all over town. I pointed to the window and said, "Welcome to the real world."

"That's not fair. You just spoiled a great day dream."

"I didn't spoil it. It is even more special because sometimes wanting can be better than having. Thoughts about what you want to have and achieve in life are always available, free, custom tailored to you, and can help you stay focused and motivated to get what you want. Use your day dreams to answer the question, 'When am I going to make the dream real?' If you are making progress toward your goal, excellent. If you aren't, this is a chance to decide if this is a day dream you enjoy experiencing but don't want to or can't make real in the foreseeable future. There's nothing wrong with having these occasionally, because you can never be sure of the future. These day dreams can keep your mind open to unexpected opportunities, but only if you are ready to see and take advantage of them."

My student relaxed a bit now, because she knew I wasn't trying to "steal her dream." All I wanted to do was put that dream in perspective. Wanting, when it's not obsessive, is very useful; it keeps you focused and motivated. You should remember to ask yourself two important questions on a regular basis. First, "Is this still what I really want?" and, "Am I still willing to do what's needed to get it?"

Finally, I told my student to beware of the thoughts and words that can mean that you're slipping from motivated to obsessed, to doing something stupid like having whatever it is before you are ready for it. I said, "Look out for thoughts like, 'I work hard every day—why shouldn't I have that?' Or, 'I deserve some joy in life just like everyone else.' Or 'All my friends have one—why shouldn't I?' Or the old standby, 'You only live once!'" Rationalizing a stupid decision with thoughts and phrases like these can make having something an absolute nightmare, instead of a day dream.

Keep dreaming and wanting and answering the questions above honestly and frequently. And remember, wanting can be better than having, especially if you aren't ready for having yet. Having what you want in life doesn't come first—preparing to get what you want comes first. Let some good constructive day dreams keep you focused and motivated, and having will be even better than the dream.

The Takeaway

- Wanting is not just what you do while you're waiting to get something. Wanting is part of what you do to prepare properly for having, so having can be better than what you dreamed it would be. That's why wanting can sometimes be better than having.

CHAPTER 28

MONEY COMES LAST

Human beings are much bigger than just making money.

MUHAMMAD YUNUS

MANY STUDENTS APPEAR IN MY office and say, "I just don't know what I want to do after graduation." Ron was one such student.

"Doc, I have a major, but I'm not sure I can be successful with it." His major was sociology.

"Now, Ron, you're asking for advice in the College of Business."

"Yes, I know, but you helped a friend of mine sort out his thoughts on this same topic, and he suggested I see you, too." Ron settled in a chair. He clearly wasn't going to leave without an answer.

"Ron, I'm flattered," I said, "but I can't tell you much about the field of sociology. Do you have a longtime interest in this area? Where's the passion?"

"I guess I do," he replied. "I like working with people, and it gives me some satisfaction, knowing I helped them."

"That sounds as if you made a good choice for a major."

Ron took a deep breath, and the truth spilled out. "Well, yes and no. What I have a real passion for is money. I want to make money."

I chuckled a bit. "Ron, the highest paying undergraduate degrees are typically in the STEM disciplines — science, technology, engineering, and mathematics. In fact, the highest paying undergraduate degree, with an average starting salary of $122,000, is petroleum engineering. Now, I'm not saying you need to become a petroleum engineer, but I do want to talk to you about money." I asked Ron whether he knew that if he did things right in life, money would come last.

"No. Doc, you don't understand — I want money to come first, not last!"

I said, "Actually money is just a tool. You can't eat it. You can't live in it. You can't drive it. Money won't keep you warm unless you burn it! It is, however, a very powerful tool. It can help you do all these things and live a rewarding life, *or* it can cause you more trouble than you can imagine. You need to find out how to use it before you earn it — not after. Having money isn't just about spending it."

"What's so complicated?" he asked, not really getting my point. "You get money, and you spend it on things you want and need. End of story. A happy ending, I might add."

"Be careful about those happy endings," I warned. "Remember, no matter how much you love things, they will never love you back. Invest your resources, including money, in meaningful experiences and on people who are important to you, without the attachment of material things."

"I still need money," Ron argued.

"Let me put it this way," I said bluntly. "Instead of buying an expensive car, buy a less expensive one and use some of the money to travel or do something else to expose yourself to interesting people in interesting places doing interesting things, to make you a more interesting person. Never stop learning and growing. That's what will keep other people interested in you and in your life—not that expensive new car." Ron looked at me, still clueless.

"Ron, you might not understand and completely appreciate what I'm saying now, but take my word for it."

At first, Ron looked as if he was about to leave. I tried to make the generational leap one more time.

"Make the money come last, after you've done all the other things," I said. "Get your education and some experience in life. Get to know yourself better, not as a student, but as a professional with a growing career in a world that you don't know much about now. Develop loving, respectful relationships with other people you can help and who can help you."

"Yeah, more than just my girlfriend," he slowly admitted.

"They may be your family, your girlfriend, friends, colleagues, or mentors. Find the people in your life who don't want to take advantage of or exploit you and who only have the highest expectations of you."

"Like my boss when I have a real job?" he asked.

"Yes, if you're lucky you'll have a boss like that," I said. "Even if your first boss is not ideal, don't lose sight of the big picture—work to add value and to be valued, to learn and in turn, teach, to offer assistance and also accept it when you need it. And remember that it is very important that you express your appreciation and gratitude for the things that come to you in life. When you do all these things well, you won't have to seek out money. Instead, it will come to you."

The Takeaway

- You can't buy the things that truly count: discipline, hard work, an open attitude, authentic experiences, and true relationships in college and beyond. It's these "priceless" attitudes and experiences that will bring money to you last, not first. They are the critical ingredients that must come first.

- Naïve notion? No. Thousands of my students live like this. You can, too. Go for it!

CHAPTER 29

COLLEGE IS JUST THE BEGINNING

Know yourself. Don't accept your dog's admiration as conclusive evidence that you are wonderful.

ANN LANDERS

I HAVE BEEN TRULY FORTUNATE IN some unexpected ways, which has offered a powerful revelation: if you work hard and you have some luck and the courage to test it, you won't always get what you think you want, but you will get what's consistent with who you truly are and what you are really good at.

One of my professors told me that I would change careers three times and change jobs seven times before I retired. Well, I am way ahead of his schedule. Millennials may job-hop twelve to fifteen times or they may be entrepreneurial and never hold a job. This may well be the new normal.

Whatever college and career hold for you in the future I want you to appreciate every experience along the way. I found that there is a secret that is key to finding your successful path through life. There is no test for it, they don't teach it in college, and only life and experience will help you discover what it is. I can tell you the secret but you're still going to have to work to find it. While you may have some help uncovering it, only you can decipher it. The secret is that you must know what you *do well* and stay open to opportunities that play to your personal strengths—that is, what you are *good at.*

It's not enough for someone to tell you this. You have to live this for yourself—through the bad, the good, and the great times and people you'll encounter. To illustrate this final takeaway and as the last story in this book, I'm going to tell you how I came to discover what I do well and what I am good at.

From the age of six, I knew what my future would be . . . or at least I thought I knew! I told anyone who would listen that I wanted to be an engineer. I dabbled in all sorts of engineering projects. I put together, painted, and customized complicated models of airplanes and cars. Then I displayed them all over my room. Yeah, yeah, I know—nerdy, but so appropriate for the engineer I planned to be! My future was set. I was the only quantitative person in my house. Everyone else had a talent for English and liberal arts and that was fine with me. I had the numbers covered, and my parents helped me with the English and writing, for which I had absolutely no patience. It seemed this plan would work well!

In high school, most of my classes were in math and science, because that was all I needed to study engineering. If a course didn't involve numbers, I just wasn't interested! My high school English teacher, Mrs. M.R. Walker, saw something in me that I didn't recognize, because of my obsession with numbers and my commitment to my career choice. Even though everything with numbers came easily to me, she said there was more to me than that.

Looking back, I knew she was right, but I just couldn't deal with it then. She would wave her arms like a windmill while saying I ought to join the debate team. I have to admit this was very entertaining, because Mrs. Walker was only five feet tall, with long arms. But she was tough. She had this "You will obey" look that could shake up even a brawny football lineman. I saw that look only two times. The first time was when I cut her class to hang out in the band room with my crew and Mrs. Walker tracked me down. All she said was, "Let's go." I immediately obeyed.

I vowed never to do anything to get the "You will obey" look again. Well, I almost made it. I saw that look one more time—when she suggested I should join the debate team. Resistance was futile. Nobody in the school, including the principal, stood a chance with Mrs. Walker when she was right.

Internally I rebelled: What was the point of words, words, words? Who was she kidding? There was nothing to calculate here. I only wanted to run the numbers!

Despite my attitude, Mrs. Walker used a combination of intimidation and persistence to wear me down. What a talent she had for hounding! She stopped me every day in the hall, "Why didn't you practice with the debate team yesterday?" Finally, she hit me with the "You must obey" look and I had no choice but to surrender! I took up extemporaneous speaking, joined the debate team, and as Mrs. Walker predicted, I was really good at it. I won every single debate I participated in, but did that really matter? No—not to me. After a year, I quit the team, because it took time away from my master plan to become an engineer.

For somebody who thought he was intellectually and visually perceptive, I was blind. I didn't want anything or anybody to distract me from my chosen path. In spite of myself, my persuasive communicator "self" would sneak out. It even helped me get elected class president my senior year of high school.

Undeterred by Mrs. Walker, or the success I had in debate and campaigning, I stubbornly marched toward my chosen road in college. I studied mechanical engineering and graduated cum laude with several engineering job offers in hand. I did not take any of them! Instead, I took a detour.

I accepted a scholarship to study for an MBA at Carnegie Mellon University. After earning that degree, I spent five years in corporate

America. I worked at several Fortune 50 firms in internal financial model building and consulting, as well as capital budgeting planning and analysis. I used my quantitative skills and my business knowledge, as expected.

Still, something was missing. I remember sitting in a meeting, while working for a Fortune 50 firm in New York, listening to my boss talk about our business as if it were a religious experience. Something felt wrong—either he was way over the top or this was not where I needed to be. As time passed, I realized both were true when the company fired Mr. Over-the-Top one Friday with no notice whatsoever. He had committed everything to the job and created a suburban lifestyle on Long Island that he now had no hope of supporting without a job. If corporate America could do this to someone so committed, someone who really towed the company line, I wondered if it was time for me to go too. I wasn't particularly happy in the corporate world but just because my boss was laid off didn't mean I couldn't be successful. Would I ever be happy in my current job or in another large corporation? Why hadn't I fulfilled my initial passion to become an engineer? I was twenty-six years old and I had no clue about my professional identity and abilities and there was no Mrs. Walker to poke, prod, and scold me into an epiphany.

As my confusion roiled, my undergraduate alma mater called, offering me the opportunity to earn a doctorate in business. I jumped at the chance, though I wasn't sure why. I just knew one thing: being a corporate analyst was not my calling.

Although I entered a very good graduate program, I was still soul searching. Then during the second year, I started teaching a course in finance—with no preparation. My only training? I had been a student! Apparently, somebody trusted me. So, armed only with a textbook and an instructor's manual, I faced the Finance 201 class for the first time. When I dismissed the class fifty minutes later, I had my epiphany! I had walked into my lifelong career the very minute I set foot in that classroom.

I stood in front of twenty-five strangers and taught them what I knew. They actually listened and learned. That was the best feedback in my work life. I loved every minute! The more I taught, the more I grew as a teacher. Every student became a personal challenge. Did I have them today? Could I see it in their faces? Did we connect? Yes, yes, and yes! The enrollment in my classes and the proficiency of my students proved it. Teaching is what I did well, but it would take more discovery to find out why, i.e., what I was really good at.

Initially, I didn't understand why I was a successful teacher. However, after spending several years in the classroom, learning my profession, and understanding its various components, I figured it out. What I was good at was speaking persuasively in public, connecting with an audience, mastering ideas and information, and then sharing that with groups larger than my classes. In short—thinking and talking! This self-discovery in my thirties changed my direction in life.

My wife, Donna, came home one evening and told me she had volunteered me to run for election on the local school board. I immediately checked her pulse and temperature because I knew she had to be delirious! She wasn't. After talking to several of my neighbors, I agreed to run for a position on the board, because I knew it was consistent with what I was really good at. Shortly after the campaign started, Donna attended one of my campaign events where I spoke. Her jaw dropped.

"You were great," she said afterward.

"That's what I do for a living," I said. "I'm a college professor!"

"It's more than that," said Donna. "You just don't speak well—you speak very persuasively."

I defeated a two-term incumbent by three votes on the fifth count of the absentee ballots! A local election landslide!

Through contacts I made serving on the board, I began international educational consulting in Africa and have since made several trips there. None of this was part of my original plan. Years before, I never could have imagined all this would happen.

THE TAKEAWAY

- You have the freedom to choose. Be open. Figure out what you do well and what you're good at. Remember, you don't have to do it by graduation day! In fact, it may take a few years to find the fit. When you find, you'll know and in the interim—be sure to enjoy the journey.

FOLLOW-UP EXERCISE

Go to **http://granvillesawyer.com/resources/** to use the **Find Your Fit** exercise. You'll see an example table that shows you how to evaluate your talents and skills in light of what you do well. An example of what is on the website is in the Appendix. Then you can fill in your own table. It's a great tool to use as you explore who you are now. Use it again in a few years as you continue that self-discovery.

A Final Take On Takeaways

Just like your time as an undergraduate, we have covered a lot of ground in *College in Four Years*. Remember, this book gives you the tools and tactics to manage the academic challenge of successfully attaining your degree. The only caveat is that *you* have to do the work we talked about here—and more. Remember I told you this was a self-indemnity policy.

I've also taken my own advice and put together an outline of the Takeaways from each chapter of *College in Four Years* to make it easier for you to keep this information top of mind. Be sure to use the resources and links I've posted online and throughout the book. You'll find a complete list in the Appendix of all of the forms and worksheets in *College in Four Years*.

While I've tried to share with you the knowledge that my students have benefited from the most, there is no way I can share everything in one book. What I can do is keep the dialogue going on my website, **www.GranvilleSawyer.com**, and on Twitter @ProfGMS, so follow me so that I can share my experiences with you and you can share your success with me.

THE TAKEAWAYS

1. Start off with the right attitude about your education, know how special college is. Statistics show that the day you start college, you have less than a fifty-six percent chance of finishing in six years and less than a twenty-five percent change of finishing in four years. Run with the big dogs (the best students) because the big dogs eat first! (Chapter 1)

2. Use the first two years of classes to try out a major before you choose it. (Chapter 2)

3. Make sure your teachers know you — be more than just a name or number. (Chapter 3)

4. Success is not automatic! Use the tips in this chapter to be successful. (Chapter 4)

5. Doing well in school is why you are in college and paying for it. Remember, your academic record will follow you for years and years after you graduate. (Chapter 5)

6. Don't cut corners to get through college; you'll only hurt yourself. In addition to not learning what you should, you're sending a strong message to anyone who knows what you did. The message is "I will lie, cheat, or steal to get what I want." And make no mistake about it, someone will know and they are going to make decisions about you as a person based on what they know. (Chapter 6)

7. When you're in college, don't try to live a life you can't afford — do the work first so you can earn the money to live the way you want. (Chapter 7)

8. Pay attention! Talk to your advisor and your teachers to know what course to take when. (Chapter 8)

9. Know how prerequisite courses will affect your course schedule — understand the prerequisites must be taken **before** other courses, not during and not after. (Chapter 9)

10. If you plan well, you will increase your commitment to success; more commitment means you will work harder and smarter to succeed; working harder and smarter will mean more success for you. (Chapter 10)

11. You can't answer questions or solve problems if you don't understand what you're doing. You can't understand what you're doing if you don't read and understand the textbook **before** trying to answer questions and solve problems. (Chapter 11)

12. The biggest difference between "A" students and everyone else is that they read the book before class — if you don't read before class, you will end up leaving class with more questions than you came in with. (Chapter 12)

13. Use your study group to test and improve the knowledge and understanding you got on your own. Remember, they can help you but they can't study for you — what the group knows is not the same as what you know; you have to get that for yourself first before your group can help you. (Chapter 13)

14. Look for coaches who can dig into the information with you and explain it clearly — in the way that you best understand. Learning how to play a valuable role in groups, as a player or coach, is one of the most important skills you can learn in college and in life. (Chapter 14)

15. You'll never know how much your teachers can help if you don't ask them. (Chapter 15)

16. Know where you stand in the class at all times. Use calculations like the example in this chapter to know what you need to get the grade you want. (Chapter 16)

17. Start working on the grade point average at graduation from the first day of class. You have no time to waste. (Chapter 17)

18. Whatever your major is, recognize the first time, the second time, the third time, and the fourth time that you see material or encounter and solve certain problems. Understand how you are supposed to master the classes and the material to each time you see it. (Chapter 18)

19. Get what you came to college for, and I don't mean grades. Get an understanding of concepts and principles so you can answer real-world questions and solve real-world problems. (Chapter 19)

20. Always ask and answer the four questions in this chapter, and you'll understand the how and why of each problem you need to solve. (Chapter 20)

21. Here's the key to coming up with answers and solutions, especially quantitative ones: read, understand the words, and then crunch the numbers. Don't try to do it the other way. It's much harder. (Chapter 21)

22. You'll have to create your own outline so it will work just for you—this takes more time and effort so be prepared to work for your success. (Chapter 22)

23. Use the outlining techniques from Chapter 21 for presentations so you won't make your class suffer through 50 of the most boring minutes of their lives while you read every slide to them one tiresome word at a time. (Chapter 23)

24. The Gut Check can work now for tests and later when you're prepping for job interviews, critical meetings, and client presentations. However, it's not a substitute for talking with your professors, mentors, and managers who can guide you when preparing for tests and other assessments of your performance in your academic and professional life. (Chapter 24)

25. Be brave enough to be happy. Pursue the experiences and goals that really interest you. Let your passion drive you, but always have a plan. (Chapter 25)

26. Pursue your passion in life but have a backup plan for times when passion doesn't pay the rent. (Chapter 26)

27. Wanting is not just what you do while you're waiting to get something. Wanting is part of what you do to prepare properly for having so having can be better than what you dreamed it would be. That's why wanting can sometimes be better than having. (Chapter 27)

28. You can't buy what counts: discipline, hard work, an open attitude, authentic experiences, and true relationships in college and beyond. It's these "priceless" attitudes and experiences that will bring money to you last, not first. (Chapter 28)

29. You have the freedom to choose. Be open. Figure out what you do well and what you're good at. Remember, you don't have to do it by graduation day! (Chapter 29)

Thank you and please let me know when graduate in four years! Email me at CI4YGrad@CreativeCache.biz

Appendix

Visit the Resources page on **www.GranvilleSawyer.com** to download interactive forms from this appendix.

Ask the Professionals:
What Was Your Post-College Plan for Success?

Set up interviews with professionals who work in your field. You will gain valuable insight into planning your own post-college experience.

1. Did you have a plan for success after college while you were in college?

2. If you did, what was it?

3. Did your plan work?

4. If it did, why did it work?

5. How much of what you did can I apply to my situation today?

6. What changes do you think I need to take into account because the business environment has changed?

7. Will you help me make a solid plan for myself, as you did?

Key Questions:
WHAT IS MY PLAN TO SUCCEED IN COLLEGE?

You have no time to waste in establishing and following a systematic plan for college. Start from day one of your freshman year. Set long-range milestones and short-range schedules.

1. **In five years, I want to have a position or start a business in** _____. This statement covers an important answer when you talk to people who are at least five years ahead of where you are.

2. **In four years, I want to** _____. When you have an idea of the goals you need to achieve by a certain deadline, you can complete this statement. Your mentors can help you answer this statement, plus the other annual goals.

3. **In three years, I want to** _____. This date moves you to a key step. Ask your mentors specifically about what they did or didn't do in college to help them work on their plan. Ask for their advice on what you should or shouldn't do.

4. **In two years, I want to** _____. Now is the time to make a final decision on a major. It is imperative that you talk with your mentors, your teachers, and your advisors about this choice. Don't rely only on your personal friends' experiences, no matter how good or bad.

5. **In one year, I want to** _____. Based on the two-, three-, and four-year goals you've already set, focus on necessary steps for the coming year: essential courses to take and other activities, such as internships (or plans for one) and

participation in professionally related groups and activities. Keep working with your mentors, teachers, and advisors because they are the most valuable resources you have. Stay on everyone's radar.

6. **In six months, I want to** _____.
You should identify this clearly, so you can follow the strategy you've laid out. Keep your advisory "team" informed of your progress. The minute you have a question, ask for guidance. Calculate the grades you need for every semester to get/keep your grade point average where it needs to be. See your instructor(s) about your calculations if you have questions. Use the "How Am I Doing?" Worksheet referenced in Chapter 16 to calculate projected grades based on estimates of scores on tests yet to be taken. A sample of the worksheet also appears on page 157. Follow up on any professional contacts you have made, to develop relationships that can lead to internships and/or jobs after graduation.

7. **In three months, I want to** _____.
With the three-month plan, evaluate expectations for the semester. Update performance calculations you did three months ago to ensure that you are still on track for your desired grades. If you need help in classes, go get it now! Follow a schedule that allows enough time to prepare for tests and turn in assignments on time. It's easy to put off semester-long projects. Avoid those last minute all-nighters! Don't wait for the end of the semester to ask for extra credit.

8. **In one month, I want to** _____.
Set goals for every month. As the semester winds down, schedule the extra study time you need to finish up long papers and prepare for exams. Meet with instructors to confirm any last-minute questions. Pre-register for courses right away. Some classes have limited enrollment, so sign up early!

9. **In one week, I want to** _____.

Break down every month, week by week. Time can move like a blur, so every Sunday, review the week's activities on your electronic calendar, paper planner, or even an old-fashioned wall calendar—use what works for *you*. Double check your log of assignments, tests, and meetings with important people.

10. **Tomorrow, I will** _____.

Base tomorrow's goals on what has to be done this week. Look at every critical hour of the day. One of my students got distracted and didn't closely check one day of activities. As a result, she missed an important informational interview and blew it with a key contact who might have helped her later in her job search. Make sure to account for every critical hour—you cannot afford to destroy relationships.

How Am I Doing Worksheet

Instructions:

COLUMN 1: Create a line for each week of class in the semester.

COLUMN 2: Insert the individual assignments, tests, projects listed on your class syllabus. Insert additional rows as needed.

COLUMN 3: List the value/weight of each of the items in Column 2 as detailed on your class syllabus.

COLUMN 4: Fill in your grades as you receive them or estimate them to project your final grade (don't forget to fill in the actual grade when you earn it).

COLUMN 5: Automatically calculates your point value for individual assignments/tests/projects giving you your average grade/ score.

COLUMN 1	COLUMN 2	COLUMN 3	COLUMN 4	COLUMN 5
From Class Syllabus	Assignments/ Tests/ Projects	Percentage/ Weight/ Value of my Total Grade	Grade Earned For This	Contribution to my Class Grade
Week 1	Homework	5%	100	5
Week 2	Homework	5%	100	5
Week 3	Midterm	25%	85	21.25
Week 4	Homework	5%	100	5
Week 5	Group Project	25%	90	22.5
	Homework	5%	100	5
	Final	30%	75	22.5
Total		100%		**86.25** Average Grade/Score

Grade Point Average Estimator

The College In Four Years Grade Point Average Estimator requires the following information:

- Your Current Grade Point Average—get this from your academic report or the registrar's office and put it in Column A

- The Number of hours you have completed toward gradua-tion—you can also get this from you academic report or the registrar—put this in Column B

- The Total Number Of Hours You Need To Graduate—get this from your academic report, the registrar or the catalog—put this in Column C

- Column D is Column C – Column B

- You then need to decide what GPA you want to graduate with—put this in Column E

- Column F is calculated as the GPA you need for the hours you have left to complete

In the first row of the table on the following page, there is a sample calculation done for a student with the following information:

- Current Grade Point Average – 2.1

- Hours Completed – 60

- Hours Needed to Complete Degree – 120

- Desired Grade Point Average At Graduation – 3.0

Example:

Current Grade Point Average	Hours Completed	Total Hours Needed For Graduation	Hours Left to Complete	Desired Grade Point Average at Graduation	Needed Grade Point for Hours Left to Complete
2.10	60	120	60	3.00	3.90

Your Calculator:

Column A	Column B	Column C	Column D	Column E	Column F
Current Grade Point Average	Hours Completed	Total Hours Needed For Graduation	Hours Left to Complete	Desired Grade Point Average at Graduation	Needed Grade Point for Hours Left to Complete
2.10	60	120	60	3.00	3.90

Important Note: The College In Four Years Grade Point Average Estimator™ is an estimate and, as such, cannot accommodate specific policies and procedures in place at all colleges and universities. Please coordinate with the registrar's office to verify exactly how your grade point average is calculated.

How to Outline Quantitative Material

The passage below is from a colleague's notes that overview a concept from algebra. It deals with solving a linear equation or an equation with only one unknown. When you're studying notes like these for a test, you can't cram every word into your head. Your outline will help you capture the key points. The steps following these notes show you how.

A linear equation is an equation that, when graphed, is a straight line. The equations have only one unknown and some constant numbers. Here is an example.

Problem in words: If you triple the distance John rode his bike (x) and subtract 9, you get 21. How far did John ride his bike?

Equivalent equation, which represents how far John rode: $3x - 9 = 21$

To solve this kind of equation, we want to put the variable x on one side of the equal sign and everything else on _____.
Once the variable is isolated, we can calculate the value of the variable. This problem and its solution follow:

1. Equation to solve:	$3x - 9 = 21$
2. Add 9 to both sides:	$3x - 9 + 9 = 21 + 9$
3. This simplifies to:	$3x = 30$
4. Divide both sides by 3:	$\dfrac{3x}{3} = \dfrac{30}{3}$
5. Simplifies to the solution:	$x = 10$

The general form of a linear equation with one variable is: $ax + b = c$

Following the same procedure (i.e., subtract b from both sides, and then divide by a), the general solution is given by $x = (c - b)/a$

When creating your outline for these notes, follow these steps:

Step *1:* Note how the professor arranges the information.

- In the passage above, he first tells you the material to be covered — linear equations — and what they are.

- He provides an example, in words and numbers/letters, of what a linear equation looks like.

- He shows you how to solve the example.

- He gives you a general form that *all* linear equations must follow.

Step *2:* Format for the outline.

- Look at the professor's notes, and choose the most important works, formulas, and numbers to include in your outline.

- Highlight them.

- Create your outline from the highlighted material. Use descending order. That is, use a roman numeral to indicate the main concept, then alphabet letters to indicate supporting details.

Example:

I. Linear Equations

A. One variable and constant numbers

B. Plots as strait line

C. General form: $ax + b = c$

D. Solve for x: $x = (c - b)/a$

This is the essence of what the professor wrote. It will key your memory so you will know how to work the problems, based on the homework and the in-class problems and discussions.

Step 3: After you have written your outline, commit it to memory.

- Practice recalling everything you know about solving these equations when you read the key on the outline. Practice, practice, practice! The recollection should become consistent, complete, and instant. You don't have time on a test to rack your brain for this information.

- You must remember everything in your outline! If you forget what your "cues" represent, everything you know about linear equations will disappear.

- Again, practice, practice, practice! You should be able to close your eyes and see the outline just as you wrote it.

Unless you study and truly understand the linear equations, your outline has no meaning. All you have done is copy down what the professor wrote. You learn nothing that way, so you will not perform well on the test. You will look at the problems but won't recognize what they are or know how to solve them.

How to Outline Non-quantitative Material

This passage is about the history of the Internet. As in the non-quantitative outline, you must isolate key words and phrases, highlight them, and boil down the information.

Development of the Internet began in the 1950s. The technology for transmitting information was developed in the 1960s and 1970s at universities and technology companies in California.

In 1982, the Internet protocol suite (TCP/IP) was standardized, and consequently, the concept of a world-wide network of interconnected TCP/IP networks, called the Internet, was introduced. Commercial Internet service providers (ISPs) began to emerge in the late 1980s and early 1990s.

The Internet was commercialized in 1995, when the last restrictions on the use of the Internet to carry commercial traffic were removed. Since the mid-1990s, the Internet has had a revolutionary impact on culture and commerce, including the rise of near-instant communication by electronic mail, instant messaging, Voice over Internet Protocol (VoIP) "phone calls," two-way interactive video calls, and the World Wide Web with its discussion forums, blogs, social networking, and online shopping sites.

The Internet's takeover of the global communication landscape was almost instant in historical terms: it only communicated 1% of the information flowing through two-way telecommunications networks in 1993, already 51% by 2000, and more than 97% of the telecommunicated information by 2007. Today, the Internet continues to grow, driven by ever greater amounts of online information, commerce, entertainment, and social networking.

This outline reduces a 200-word passage to a streamlined summary that will cue information needed to answer test questions. Think of each item (A–F) as a sentence or thought that you will write on your test. If you forget the item, you will forget that all-important sentence. Practice, practice, practice.

The Internet

A. Started in 1950s
B. Further developed in 1960s and 1970s
C. 1982: TCP/IP
D. 1980s–1990s: ISPs
E. Impact: email, IM, VoIP, video calls, WWW, blogs, social networking, online shopping
F. Global Communications: 1993 — 1%; 2000 — 51%; 2007 — 97%

Find Your Fit

Use this three-step exercise to get an idea of the talents and skills that you use frequently to do things well. This exercise will help figure out your fit (e.g., what you do well matched to your natural skill and attributes). Here is my own example:

What I'm Good at and What I Do Well

Step One: What I Did Well	*Step Two:* The Skills and Talents I Used
1. Developed and delivered training for online computer applications	Communicating Motivating Explaining
2. Helped student groups prepare for business plan competition	Listening Communicating Motivating
3. Set up flat screen television and audio with critical input from my wife	Following directions Thinking critically Listening Communicating Understanding
4. Developed the concept for *College in Four Years*	Understanding concepts Seeing new relationships Communicating new ideas
5. Developed the curriculum for graduate students in finance	Organizing Motivating Communicating

6. Persuaded other faculty members to support and implement the finance curriculum I developed	Listening Learning Understanding Interpreting Communicating Motivating Self-confidence
7. Learned the ins and outs of blogging	Willingness to learn Willingness to take risk Self-confidence
8. Effectively explained complex financial concepts to students	Listening Understanding Interpreting Communicating
9. Helped my daughter through high school (with honors) and into a very good college	Planning Discipline Consistency
10. Completed a two-year computer application development project on time and within budget	Planning Consistency Discipline Understanding and application of management concepts

Step Three: Identify and count skills, talents, and experiences:

- Things listed four or more times are strong indicators of what I'm good at: communicating, motivating, listening.

- Anything listed between two and four times may be related to what I'm good at: explaining, learning, understanding, planning, consistency, discipline, self-confidence.

- Anything listed fewer than two times may be related to what I'm good at, but I do not use them frequently.

Use this form to find your fit.

What I'm Good At and What I Do Well

Step One: What I Did Well	*Step Two:* The Skills and Talents I Used
1.	
2.	
3.	
4.	
5.	
6.	
7.	
8.	
9.	
10.	

Step Three: Identify skills, talents, and experiences:

- Things listed four or more times are strong indicators of what you're good at.

- Anything listed between two and four times may be related to what you're good at.

- Anything listed fewer than two times may be related to what you are good at, but aren't being used frequently.

NOTES

NOTES

NOTES

NOTES

CPSIA information can be obtained at www.ICGtesting.com
Printed in the USA
LVOW04s2245051015

457071LV00012B/184/P